# Gay Travels
# in the Muslim World

# Gay Travels
# in the Muslim World

Michael T. Luongo
Editor

Routledge
Taylor & Francis Group
New York   London

For more information on this book or to order, visit
http://www.haworthpress.com/store/product.asp?sku=5481

or call 1-800-HAWORTH (800-429-6784) in the United States and Canada
or (607) 722-5857 outside the United States and Canada

or contact orders@HaworthPress.com

Published by

Harrington Park Press®, the trade division of The Haworth Press, Inc., 10 Alice Street, Binghamton, NY 13904-1580.

PUBLISHER'S NOTE
The development, preparation, and publication of this work has been undertaken with great care. However, the Publisher, employees, editors, and agents of The Haworth Press are not responsible for any errors contained herein or for consequences that may ensue from use of materials or information contained in this work. The Haworth Press is committed to the dissemination of ideas and information according to the highest standards of intellectual freedom and the free exchange of ideas. Statements made and opinions expressed in this publication do not necessarily reflect the views of the Publisher, Directors, management, or staff of The Haworth Press, Inc., or an endorsement by them.

Cover photos by Michael T. Luongo: King Abdullah Mosque in Jordan; Petra valley in Jordan; Border between Palestine and Jordan with mileage points to biblical sites.

Cover design by Kerry Mack.

**Library of Congress Cataloging-in-Publication Data**

Gay travels in the Muslim world / Michael T. Luongo, editor.
    p. cm.
    Includes bibliographical references.
    ISBN: 978-1-56023-339-8 (hard : alk. paper)
    ISBN: 978-1-56023-340-4 (soft : alk. paper)
    1. Gays—Travel—Islamic countries. 2. Islamic countries—Description and travel. I. Luongo, Michael.

    HQ75.26.I74 G39 2007
    910.86'64091767—dc22

                                                                        2006036546

For those who helped who prefer to be anonymous.

# CONTENTS

# Foreword

When my friend Michael Luongo asked me to write a Foreword to this book, I felt quite honored. In any other situation I might have felt insulted. It is that whole "Oh, shit, I'm being used by The White Man for the exploitation of my own people" idea. But you see, I came to know about the book long before he even sent the first submission call. Michael, at the time, was working on his first book in the "Out in the World" series.

When Michael told me about his desire to put a book such as this together, I kind of felt scared, to be honest. It has been the practice of Western travel writers to somehow always make exotic whatever other people they wrote about, and certainly very few would argue that any other people have been more victimized by this practice than Muslims, for so long.

For the longest time, Europe did not take Muslims seriously. Even when Muslims were conquering many Christian-ruled lands in the Middle East and North Africa, Christendom thought, "Nah, not those people. They can't hurt a fly. They are too primitive." It would be a long time before Christendom realized we were real people and that our old civilizations were neither dead nor forgotten by us.

At the same time, Michael is a friend, and I know the kind of person he is. I know very well he is not the kind of Western traveler who will exploit my people. I guess it was because he wrote about travel issues in the Muslim world for *Huriyah* and for other publications. His travel writings in post–9/11 Afghanistan, Turkey, and the Arab world always left me educated about the current climate and situations of my own Muslim brothers and sisters.

*Gay Travels in the Muslim World*
© 2007 by The Haworth Press, Inc. All rights reserved.
doi:10.1300/5481_a

However, what really pushed me to accept the project was that many (queer) Muslims contributed. It was not going to be "those" books. It was going to be a book of travel stories in the Muslim world by Muslims as well as non-Muslims. This book was certainly not going to be any ordinary book. I knew it would become something I would be proud to be part of.

Some of the stories ring true for me. Others are of unfamiliar experiences. But they are all really wonderful. The kohl-eyed, with a *gutra* on his head, topped off with an *aghal*, Western-born brother Rahal, in his piece "Full Moon in AlAin," brings an immediate and erotic image of what was worn by many of the boys I met in the Arabian peninsula. There is something intoxicatingly beautiful about an Arab man who paints his eyes with kohl. It is not that he is a drag queen or even feminine, but the mixture of his masculinity and the touch of (external) femininity makes an affront of sorts in the culture, which I find beautiful, for everything "abnormal" is beautiful to me.

Both being either Muslim or gay is unique. But this brings me to a question: Why is it that people who don't even know us consider our stories and lives and desires and choices abnormal? It amazes me to no end that heterosexual scholars have the audacity to pass judgment in their (ever-condemning) fatwa about our sexualities. The only answer that I can think of is that they don't know us. And the only way I can think of to change this is for us to help them get to know us. After all, ignorance is bliss. And, damn it, with that ugly cliché in my mind let's continue to disrupt that bliss!

Over the past couple of decades, queer Muslims have gained a visibility that we just did not have for a long time. The 1990s was a decade in which many movements came together. Queer Muslims marched in Turkey, asking for their rights. Support groups and organizations from all corners of the world, such as Salaam, Al-Fatiha, Lambda Istanbul, and Al-Fitrah, all opened their doors. Clerics and scholars from our own communities, such as brother Muhsin Hendricks of South Africa, sister Ghazala Anwar of the United States, and brother Omar Nahas of the Netherlands, all were out and about and spoke about their faith and sexuality.

In 2000, I founded *Huriyah,* the world's first magazine for queer Muslims. With four friends from four corners of the world, although it took us a year to finally launch, this labor of love now has a worldwide English version (available free of charge from the Internet) and an Arabic version that reaches nineteen countries. When my friend Abu Omar in Egypt asked me, "How are we going to reach all these people?" referring to the estimated more than 150 million queer Muslims around the world, he underestimated the hunger of queer Muslims to be aware of one another all over the world. In less than three years, the magazine gained over 253 people in 72 countries.

I hope that *Gay Travels in the Muslim World* will be another sweet addition to the wonderful disruption of many Muslim people's bliss of ignorance about the struggles to reconcile who we gay Muslims among them are and their ever-present objection to and rejection of our existence. And I hope that they can find it in their hearts to be content with such disruption.

Afdhere Jama
*Huriyah* magazine

# Preface: Homosexuality and Coverage of the Islamic World

I was raised in an America that taught me to hate Muslims. When I was in grade school I was shown pictures of dead Israeli babies, blown up by terrorists and told, "This is what Muslims do." Vanessa Redgrave was vilified in the same classrooms, as the very example of evil for supporting the Palestine Liberation Organization and Arafat perform their horrific deeds. Beyond these unofficial injections by teachers of their opinions into the curriculum, there was of course the photograph of Malcolm X in our history books, a black Muslim whom we were taught professed violence against whites. He was contrasted against the peace loving, and obviously very Christian, Reverend Martin Luther King Jr. The photographs and explanations of the differences between these two civil rights leaders, made clear by their religious affiliations, only served to justify the words of my teachers in the minds of us pliable young students.

Certainly, the white ethnic makeup of my neighborhood, largely Jews and Catholics, played a huge role in this curriculum. The conservative and prejudiced Italians and Irish might have finally reached their long sought professional nirvana, but all still felt the sting of their sordid working-class upbringings, which lurked precariously around the corner from furniture-less houses bought on overextended credit. They needed an enemy. Jewish playmates in the neighborhood

*Gay Travels in the Muslim World*
© 2007 by The Haworth Press, Inc. All rights reserved.
doi:10.1300/5481_b

always had visits from Brooklyn-based grandparents who had survived the Holocaust. Everyone had cousins and uncles and aunts living on kibbutzim, eking out a living in a fragile Israel little more than three decades old. Swords weren't beaten into plowshares there, though; the two were worshipped side by side. Living rooms were adorned with photographs of relatives who had guns in one hand, farm implements in the other. The Israeli-Palestinian Conflict, the oil embargo, the Iran Hostage Crisis, all of these issues were alive and well in my classroom and in my neighborhood, with Arabs and Muslims the enemy all around no matter whether we were Jews or Catholics.

The indoctrination of this philosophy—the idea that these people of the desert lived in mysterious and evil ways—was part of the curriculum in my grade school. We were taught that these people who ran around with rags on their heads were a dangerous threat to our American way of life. This was a world and a people I had never met, and had no way of knowing, other than through the images in my teacher's hand, the messages in her voice, and the words on the blackboard and in our school books, that were reified by the images at home on television. And I grew up not in a backward place, but in suburban New Jersey, a short ride from Manhattan, the most diverse place in all of the world. Yet on matters Muslim, there seemed little in the way of understanding. Between school and television and community, there was no way when I was a child to like or understand the truth of what a Muslim was.

This was of course not always the case. Other teachers seemed more open on the subject, even if their discussions wavered between alarm and enlightenment. After the gasoline crisis, some teachers discussed the Arabic world in terms of money and power, and a need to realign ourselves, to conserve, to perhaps not be so militant. This was mostly a way of thinking that came along when Jimmy Carter became president. Yet, I remember also a conversation about art auctions at Sotheby's where, with gasoline prices so high, I was told that Arabs were buying European and American art in record amounts. One teacher advised that we should go to museums to see our Western art before it was all snatched away by these desert marauders, hidden away along with their veiled women in their new gilded palaces. All of this luxury, it was made clear to us, was bought at the expense of our time waiting in gas lines.

Other teachers taught us the Arabic way of life, about the art and culture that paved the way for the Renaissance, about words in English derived from this language we could never fathom. One year, we children put a world play on stage. I volunteered to be the Arab, since the teacher could not assign someone to be one with such tensions ever present. I remember loving how I looked with a turban, a ragged piece of cloth over my mouth, only my eyes visible, the cloth and my thick eyelashes accenting them, the white robe contrasting with my black hair. It was a style with which I think I did well, even as a child of eight or nine or ten years old. I felt I looked like a miniature Lawrence of Arabia, though it would be years before I understood better the even deeper implications of that comparison. I remember how we all marched on stage presenting what we were and where we were from when we performed this world parade before our parents. But when it came time for the Arab to get his accolades, for me to be the center of attention among all the make-believe ethnic groups, barely an adult beyond my parents and the teachers cared to clap. I was taught, in a very painful way, at a very young age, the risk I would put myself in if I thought to defend the Muslim and Arab way of life.

It should not be a surprise then that I grew up afraid of anything tinged with the hint of being Muslim or Middle Eastern—the people especially. This prejudice followed me into my early adult life, but always became a push and a pull between my intense natural curiosity and this terribly racist ideology into which I had been indoctrinated. My first time ever meeting and attempting to converse even relatively openly about these issues was in a beauty salon in Los Angeles. The woman who took care of me was incredibly beautiful, and I knew from her thick black hair and from her accent that she probably was Middle Eastern. When I asked where she was from, she explained that she was Persian, and I asked for clarification. She must have meant she was Iranian; Persia had disappeared a long time ago. *Persian* she insisted, but she wanted to discuss nothing further with me on the topic, nothing about where she was from and nothing of the revolution and the embassy takeover. Nothing. This was the mid 1980s, only a few short years after all of the turbulence. I felt sorry for her, as if she were worried that I might do something to her, that she might embody all that had gone wrong between our two countries and that I might hate her for what she was and where she was from. Even then, though, I knew that Iranians were not Arabic, and this too made me feel more comfortable around her. Still, I felt bad that she would not talk more on the subject, that I could not slate my curiosity, that I could not extract from her all the information about her region that I was denied from hearing firsthand, unfiltered by politics and prejudice, for my entire life.

But I was not always so curious about people who were different, who were Muslim. I still continued to be afraid, and how could you blame me, considering my background, considering all I had been taught? I remember being on a campus bus at my school, Rutgers University, which prides itself on its diversity, yet which seemed, at least while I was there, to offer few ways for different groups to properly interact with one another in a meaningful way. I was waiting for the bus to leave when another student, a Pakistani, got on. He was an angry young man, angry at the way the world perceived him, and he was trying to do something about it. He was posting signs on the bus about Muslims not being terrorists, and he was calling on people like me to come to an event to learn more about the way we thought about people like him. I looked at him however not as the person he was in front of me, but through the two decades of prejudice that had been instilled in me and I panicked. What if the flyers and the calls to educate were all a plot? What if he had a bomb? Under a Reagan-Bush administration of extremism, Muslim militancy was on the rise in Europe. Maybe he was a terrorist trying to throw me off his trail, trying to hijack this bus, take us all on his suicide mission? He handed me a flyer, looked directly at me with his intense eyes, and I ran off the bus for fear of my life. The bus didn't explode or get hijacked, but because of my irrational fears, I was late for class.

My homosexuality and my fear of Muslims came together at a notorious campus cruising area known as Seminary Place, technically a Catholic institution separate from the University, but completely surrounded by it. From my freshman year on, I had gone there to meet other closeted gay college men like myself, some with whom I still remain good friends. We'd watch as priests would one night run all the gay people off the property, or the next night wait in the bushes with them, on their knees in a position that had nothing to do with prayer or the body of Christ. During the years that I used the place, there was a tall, handsome Arab student who also cruised the paths and bushes. But I was always afraid of him. I still remember the earnestness in his face as he would try to interact with me along the pathways, and on the staircase that climbed up the hill to the seminary. I would say hello back, politely but nervously, and continue on my way. What was I so afraid of? What would he do with me? Why were my fears merely based on assumptions of what he was and what his ethnicity and religion were? I knew nothing more about him than what I assumed based on appearances, and because of this, I learned nothing more about him. I still can clearly recall him in my mind as I write this. He was handsome enough for me to want sexually, but his ethnicity and all my assumptions kept me away.

Still, it was in college that I began to realize, that although this man was someone I was very attracted to and yet afraid of, I did not feel the same about every Middle Eastern man. I don't remember his name, but there was a swarthy, devastatingly handsome Lebanese guy in some of my classes whom I knew only on the most casual basis. One day, a Lebanese event was being held at the student center, and never having seen a collection of Arabic people together at once, and noticing as well that many of the men, like the student in my classes, were very handsome, I decided to venture in. My own dark, Italian features meant, as they had since I was a child, that I could easily pass as Arab myself, and not so immediately feel out of place. I shyly tried to mingle, and while sampling pastries prepared with rose water, I ran into my friend. (To this day, anything rose water always brings him to mind.) He was happy to see me, if not a little surprised. I was confused between the curiosity of my mind, which wondered so much about his culture, and that of the curiosity centered below my belt, which wondered about his sexuality and what this darkly handsome young friend might be like in bed. I never learned the answer to that, but I did attend a few more Lebanese student events with him over the years. Yet while religion never came up in conversation, I knew enough about Lebanese refugees from the war that most were Catholics, and so I rarely had the fear of the Lebanese that I had of other Arabs. Certainly by now I knew too, that something about Arab and Middle Eastern men appealed to me on a deeper, sexual level. My homosexuality, and my curiosity about the culture, still tempered by lingering prejudices instilled within me as a child, were all fighting against one another internally. I wasn't sure yet what side would win.

So this is the background of my upbringing and of my own early intense prejudices against Muslims, which will probably come as a surprise to most people who know my work on travel in the Islamic world for both gay and mainstream publications. But you see, while I was coming to terms with my own prejudices, realizing how ridiculous they were as my travels in the Muslim world continued, I grew as a person. By directly experiencing various Middle Eastern, Arab and Muslim cultures on their own turf with my own eyes, I began to break down my own prejudices, a living example of the cliché about the power of travel to broaden one's mind. Of course, in the midst of all of this, the defining event of our time, September 11th, occurred, changing everything about travel, my specialty, and the relations between the Christian West and Islamic East. The crisis meant that I as a writer had to impart my thoughts on the subject to a greater audience, and to my own particular audience, gay men who love to travel. The very hands that type these words dug through the rubble of the Twin Towers, looking for dead bodies. After doing such a thing, all I can ever want in this world is peace and understanding between East and West, but I have no other skill to offer toward that goal than writing my own positive experiences within a culture that so many others paint as evil.

In addition, this book owes its existence also to a curious phenomenon I discovered when I was putting together my first Haworth book, *Between the Palms,* a well-reviewed collection of literary gay travel erotica. Ironically, it was on September 11th itself that I first laid eyes on the contract for that book, after coming home from a flight at 2:00 a.m., which was the last time I ever saw the Twin Towers from the windows of a plane. In fact, I barely saw them through the window. In a strange premonition, clouds from the torrential rainstorm of September 10th still hung over the World Trade Center at that time, obscuring the Twin Towers, making me gasp in my airplane seat as if even at that moment, they had already vanished from sight, hours before they actually would.

When I called for submissions for *Between the Palms,* I was surprised that more than a third of the stories I received involved either gay men's travels within, as Condoleezza Rice puts it, the Greater Middle East, or about their experiences with Muslim men who had migrated to and felt marooned in other countries. Gay men had a deep connection to these places, and they had a strong desire to tell of their travels and interactions with Muslim men. Many other men wanted to read about it. Because of this, and because of the greater problems between East and West, I decided to do this book. There is an unmet need and desire in our turbulent times to look at travels in the Muslim world and the Middle East through the eyes of gay men, both Muslim and non-Muslim.

My wish to put this book together did not exist in a vacuum, or as a strange quirk within my own imagination. Ever since September 11th, homosexuality and its relation to world turmoil and Islamic tradition have been together in the news all over the place. Depending on what you read, Islamic attitudes toward homosexuality are even a cause of the problems we find ourselves in today.

Mohammed Atta is clearly a case in point. This infamous and socially awkward young man, a self-hating homosexual by some lurid newspaper accounts, was compelled in part by internalized homophobia to drive a plane into the Twin Towers, setting in motion the world turbulence we are experiencing today. Look at his photos, some accounts stated, how weak and skinny, and therefore gay, he appeared to be. Of course, he had masculinity issues and something to prove, so why not become a terrorist, slam a plane into a building, and show the world you're not the faggot your father thinks you are? Such an explanation is to me is beyond ridiculous and insulting, but whether Atta's homosexuality is true or not, according to Jerry Falwell, the very existence of gays and lesbians caused God to command that September

11th happen. Homosexuality has been part of the discussion from the very beginning of this conflict. Someone else started it. I'm only adding some intelligent thought to the conversation.

The Taliban forces whom we conquered so easily in Afghanistan after September 11th might have famously pushed walls on sodomites and other people they deemed sinners, but it was clear that man-on-man love was something they practiced among themselves. The Taliban came from the Kandahar region of Afghanistan, so well known for its association with homosexuality that a famous Afghan legend states birds fly over the city with one wing, protecting their backsides from possible penetration. Like many religious groups, the Taliban liked to practice what they preached against. Being established in Kandahar, it would be the same as a conservative religious group here in the United States placing its headquarters in West Hollywood; they would eventually have to allow many behaviors they said they were against, otherwise no one would join. So close was this connection that even the men's fashion magazine *Details* had a cover headline about gay practices among the Taliban.

By now, my writings on Afghanistan looking at homosexuality—ancient, modern, open, and forbidden—within that country are well known to my reading audience. I have documented them in one way or another in New York's *Gay City News, Genre, Passport, Out Traveler,* and more. I suppose that if I died tomorrow, these writings would be the thing that in my life I was most remembered for. And I would be smiling down from the heavens for such thoughts. Any Google search will find these articles, as well as those written by straight journalists who were repulsed by Afghan homosexuality, as in Scotland's *Scotsman,* or by female journalists who could sensitively ask questions on the topic but only delve just so far into the issues, such as in the *Los Angeles Times.*

Even the circumstances of the death of one of the most controversial Arab leaders of our time is tinged with homosexuality. Rumors have abounded for years that Yasser Arafat was gay, and supposedly evidence exists for sexual encounters recorded by spies who kept an eye on him. With his estranged and much younger wife at his side, he died in Paris of a mysterious blood illness which, though one of his doctors described as idiopathic thrombocytopenic purpura, still led to discussions of what other "blood illnesses" it might have been. It may be years before we know if AIDS was the cause of his death or not, as some rumors put it. If it is indeed true that one of the greatest figures of terror to the Western world was gay, what would that mean for gay rights issues throughout the Middle East? Still, the practice, not the identity, is what is tolerated in the Middle East. The same rumors abound for other Muslim politicians and leaders within current conflict zones, not all of which have appeared in print, to the best of my knowledge, so therefore, I will not repeat them.

Certainly, the most lurid and sensational connection between homosexuality and an America at war with the Middle East is the Abu Ghraib scandal. A few paragraphs in this book cannot even begin to do justice to the complexities at issue on the subject. Homosexuality, and "gay" treatment in prison was itself considered torture by the American military system. One has to wonder the sick mind-set of prison guards who run around with the mentality of fraternity brothers, devising forms of coercion and torture usually done only on college campuses. How such torture can be construed and in essence defended is as sick as the torture itself. Yet, even this appalling behavior, which, in severe violation of the Geneva Conventions, put every American at risk, whether a soldier on the battleground or those of us here on the home front, was dismissed by some as the work of a U.S. military that needed to ban gay men from its service. If assumedly straight prisoners were tortured this way by what I believe were straight male and female soldiers (who court records indicate had sex with one another after torturing prisoners), one can only imagine how badly gay Muslim prisoners might have been treated by the military. Keep in mind that at the root of the torture is not the Middle Eastern view that homosexuality is degrading, but the American view that it is.

Indeed, I know how homosexuality and American perceptions of it have been used against us, even in countries where the practice is well accepted. Such was the case in Afghanistan, where following the Abu Ghraib incident and just before Karzai's 2004 election, U.S. soldiers were accused of raping their Afghan translators, and a gay Westerner working to uncover corruption was jailed by the Afghan government in a gay witchhunt. It is not that Afghans care about men having sex with men, in fact I know personally how well accepted it is within Afghan culture. Instead, Afghans who did not want Karzai in power knew Americans fear homosexuality and used our prejudices to embarrass us and try, unsuccessfully, to derail his election. Yet, while bombs and kidnappings make the news, these complex issues in this faraway nation did not, and you will find none of this discussed in any U.S. newspaper (though it was covered in the UK). In fact, U.S. publications, gay and straight, with which I discussed the topic refused to cover it. This issue, which clearly showed how Abu Ghraib can directly be used against us, was deemed simply not worth covering.

Many other examples of this fusion of conflict and homosexuality during our war with the Middle East exist. One is the strange story of the Iraqi terrorists in the north of the country who murdered people and then filmed themselves having gay sex with one another. The tapes were even shown on Iraqi television. We also read in gay and straight newspapers, especially in the detailed and groundbreaking coverage by Doug Ireland in the New-York-based *Gay City News,* of the hangings of gay teenagers in public squares. In our own country, and putting the U.S. at greater risk in the war on terrorism, Arabic language experts translating possible attack messages continue to be fired simply because they are gay. What new 9/11 will occur because of this senseless policy, when we don't have enough of such people working for the government to begin with?

So from the very beginning of this conflict, a war of religious ideology by both Bible and Koran thumpers, homosexuality has been intertwined throughout all of the issues and all of the main events, whether it is New York, Kabul, Iraq, Guantanamo, or Palestine. So what I present to you here, after all this exposition, both personal and political, is a book that looks at homosexuality, Islam, and the world we find ourselves in now, and finds mostly joy, all seen through the personal experiences of gay men in the United States, Europe, and from the Middle East and South Asia as well.

There are many, both Muslims and non-Muslims alike, who have told me that I am exploiting these issues in too sexual a way, or that I am exoticizing Muslims into sexual caricatures, that I do not understand the complexities of the region. I will leave you to be the judge. You may or may not agree with these assessments, but I ask you to read all of the stories in this volume before jumping to any conclusions, before making any assumptions. I expect that you will not agree with all of the works in this volume either, for each of these authors takes a very different view of his travels within Islamic regions of the world. I myself do not agree with all of the authors in this book, many of whom are fellow Westerners who had vastly different experiences from mine, or those of Middle Eastern heritage whose mind-set and emotional state visiting their places of heritage I can never place myself into. Some authors find love and a singular attraction, even a husband of sorts. Others find sex tinged with violence, all of it coming at an expensive price of either money or life or both. Some Muslims who return to their homelands find warmth and a desire for social change and acceptance; others would rather never set foot in their birthplaces again. Each man has a different story to reflect his individual experience. Each is a unique window into this seemingly closed world, which, if you come with a curious mind, opens itself to outsiders very quickly, contrary to popular belief.

Some will also argue with me about where I stand with human rights. I believe all people deserve equal rights and equal treatment, regardless of their orientation. I also believe, however, that a tremendous difference exists between how homosexuality is expressed in the Western world and in the Islamic world, and this is where the conflict begins. To simplify a very complex issue, in Europe and America and places under Western influence, homosexual desire and acts become the very definition of a person, they create an identity that separates him or her from the rest of society. In much of the Islamic world, homosexual desire and acts are simply one aspect among others, something people do but not something that defines a person above all other traits. It is when the Western model of identity challenges this Eastern thought that the problems begin. I doubt the day will come when gay people will march through Kabul's Chicken Street with rainbow flags in their hands. If it ever does, that would be wonderful. What I think is more interesting, more natural perhaps, is that I can wander into gardens near mosques and have men make jokes about bananas and asses with flirtatious glances as they try to chat with me, and yet none would have any idea what a gay Pride parade is.

Within many of these cultures, to do is not to be, though clearly there are men who would be gay in every sense of the Western word. Homosexuality is something natural, something men do and enjoy with each other, yet it is not the basis of identity as it is in the West. What many try to do is create a Western paradigm within these cultures, and it is this that creates the backlash. Does the Arab world need gay bars where men pay too much for pink drinks and listen to disco divas just like in the West ? The Middle East does not need such things, and fears such things; it is the model of Western decadence, and it goes beyond the notion of simply homosexuality. Unfortunately, this is part of the dilemma and the problem with the Cairo 52, the gay Egyptian men who were on a Nile boat that doubled as a gay bar, too strong a Western influence according to the government. Clearly, though, this is a human rights issue if there ever was one. It shows the odd but terrible push and pull in a country that for thousands of years has sanctified homosexuality, but fears its commercialization in the Western sense, even though Egypt has by now been strongly influenced by Europe. But if men want to lie in the desert sands and make love to one another, only the full moon and their camels as witnesses, no one in the Middle East gives a damn. And it has been this way in the Middle East since the dawn of time and civilization, and will remain so long after our Western society has collapsed on itself.

Much of the writing for this book has been done by Kafirs, or people who are not Muslim, men such as myself, but who, through their travels, have gained an understanding of Muslim countries. One of my favorite lines of all comes from the blond, blue-eyed, and very European Stevens's "I Want Your Eyes," in which he describes his interactions wandering an Arabian city, unsure if he is being cruised, objectified, hated, or about to be robbed. All such feelings might come to any gay Westerner in the Muslim world, partly as a result of reality, partly because he might stand out, and most of all, because of the seeming cognitive dissonance between the Western view of what the Islamic world is like and its actual reality. The story reads like poetry with the line, "our cultures lapping at each other like the waves in the harbor" among my favorite of all of them.

For Westerners in such cultures, there is often an incredible sense of loneliness. Having been an expat myself, albeit it in another culture, I have read few things that capture this sense better than British Des Ariel's "Little Stints." His story is one of isolation, of not feeling that he is part of the British or American culture with which he sometimes must surround himself or a part of the larger Arabic culture he works in. Yet, it is within the native culture that he finds solace, often sexually, even if he feels he is something like a "service station" to the sexual appetites of handsome young men in bedouin gear. He had once fallen in love, but the man left long ago, and much of the story involves trying to get back that feeling. In the end of the story he seems to be on some kind of suicide mission, or perhaps he is only thrill seeking. It's interesting and breathtaking to read as the story unfolds.

Rahal's piece tells of a different situation, of someone who is Muslim, but a free spirit around the world in many cultures and countries. He mentions "unity within diversity" under Islam, something I wish that the Christian Right in America could understand and embrace. His story, part of a larger work, tells of what it is like to be from one Muslim country and live and work in another, interacting with both Western expats and other Muslims alike.

The rest of the stories remain a mix of so many different experiences. Although it is true that some of the Westerners offer stories of cultural confusion, and perhaps not going under the surface, baffled by the differences, many go deeper into the clash of cultures. Thomas Bradbury's story in Turkey tells of a Westerner who finds love through compromise, in spite of a very culturally confused beginning. Some stories, like "My Intifada" by Ethan Pullman, are deeply disturbing, and speak of the problems that can exist for a young man growing up gay in the Middle East, even when he takes flight at an early age, escaping to the United States.

I now invite you as the reader to come along with me, whether you are gay, straight, Muslim, or a Kafir like me who has taken a long journey to overcome prejudice. Join me and the writers I have collected on this journey of understanding, and, like me, overcome the prejudices and the hatred that decades of media and American educa-tion might have instilled within you. Hold my hand, as you would be allowed to hold any other man's hand on the streets of an Islamic city in a way you would be ridiculed for in Europe and America. Come with me, and follow me into the pages of this book.

# Acknowledgments

I want to thank Bill Cohen and Bill Palmer for being so supportive of the unusual gay travel work I wanted to do for this book, *Gay Travels in the Muslim World,* my second in the Harrington Park Press series "Out in the World." I also want to thank Jay Quinn for his support and guidance, which has helped to form the basis for my understanding of how to run a series of my own. Special thanks also must go out to Rebecca Browne of Haworth, whom I have known for many years and whom I got to finally meet during the work for this book. I also must give her thanks for her constant concern and worry during my Afghanistan research for the book. I also must thank Robert, Margaret, Paul, and everyone else at Haworth for all of their support with my many questions, ideas, lateness, and other mishaps. Thanks also goes to Rose Arce for her help with contacts. As usual, thanks to my roommates Harry and Khoa for putting up with my late-night editing habits that keep them awake, and for keeping track of my mail while I travel. For my contributors who have to put up with my own disorganization and e-mails saying "Wait till I am back in the U.S." So many thanks must also go to my various editors at the publications I work for, with Paul Schindler especially for his allowing me to do a series of articles about gay travel in Islamic regions for *Gay City News,* which helped to form the basis of this book. For Bill Henning who saw the value of my work in Kandahar for *Genre* magazine, and to Matt Link for his support of my work when he was at *Out Traveler,* and to Andrew Mersmann at *Passport* for his support as well. Thanks for my friend Syed who took me around much of Kandahar and translated for me and who overcame his own misconceptions about homo-

*Gay Travels in the Muslim World*
© 2007 by The Haworth Press, Inc. All rights reserved.
doi:10.1300/5481_c

sexuality through our work together. Congratulations on your asylum in the United States. To an Afghan-American mother-and-son team who were phenomenally helpful with my work in Afghanistan, but who probably prefer to be anonymous. For Ingrid Breyer, who, as always, remains a dear friend and colleague in my travel work and a sounding board for all of my problems and issues. For Asha for all her interest in my work in print and image in this region. And, of course, to all the men in Condoleezza's "Greater Middle East" who have shared their lives and thoughts with me, this strangely curious Kafir, over the years. I can never thank you all enough.

# ✵ 1    It All Began with Mamadou

*Jay Davidson*

How did I, a "nice Jewish boy," come to live in an Islamic republic? And what kind of life did I have there? It's a tale that demonstrates not only the rewards of lifelong learning, but also the necessities of not falling victim to stereotypes promoted by the media.

I was fifty-four years old when I applied to join the Peace Corps, setting into motion the fulfillment of a dream I'd had since President John F. Kennedy started the organization, when I was an impressionable adolescent. While waiting for my interview with the Peace Corps recruiter, I spied the Lesbian, Gay, and Bisexual Returned Peace Corps Volunteers' newsletter on display in the reception area. Encouraged by what appeared to be a supportive organization, I came out to the recruiter by letting her know of the triple distinction I had, which might make a difference in my placement: that I was a gay Jewish vegetarian, and fully intended to remain all three during my service.

I came to find out that the Peace Corps does a fine job in matching the skills, interests, and needs of its applicants to the requests of host country governments. I told my recruiter that wherever I went I wanted to be in the largest city possible. Not for me was the village life in which all the inhabitants knew my every movement—what I ate for breakfast, when I cut my toenails, where I went when I left the house and, to be frank, who visited me in my home and for how long he stayed.

Much to my surprise, the recruiter's greatest concern was with my vegetarianism. In order for my application to be considered, I was required to sign an agreement to the effect that I would not incite an international incident by refusing to eat any critter that had been

*Gay Travels in the Muslim World*
© 2007 by The Haworth Press, Inc. All rights reserved.
doi:10.1300/5481_01

slaughtered in my honor. She also posited that she would be able to minimize such a scenario by placing me in a large city, where I could live more or less anonymously, which is what I wanted anyway.

As my application advanced, I learned that I would be going to West Africa, where there was a critical need for men who spoke French. When the invitation arrived, I had to give myself a geography lesson, for I had never even heard of Mauritania. I looked on a world map that was bordered by flags of every country. When I recognized on Mauritania's flag the star and crescent that appears on the flags of many Islamic nations, my first sensation was queasiness, an unsettling and nauseous feeling in my stomach. Maybe this placement wasn't such a smart idea! It was just one year after September 11, 2001, and Muslims were widely being portrayed by the media as militant fundamentalists, and not welcoming to Americans, let alone gay people and Jews. Yet at the same time it did not occur to me that upon retiring from teaching I would take it easy at home in San Francisco, enjoying all there was to offer in what many consider to be the global epicenter of gay life.

It took only a day, though, for a calmness to wash over me, replacing my anxiety. My inner voice—the one I had learned to trust when it spoke—told me, "Accept the invitation. You will teach what you need to teach and learn what you need to learn." It was with that leap of faith that I plunged into the maelstrom of activity to prepare for both my retirement from teaching and leaving home for two years.

During the month that preceded our departure, nineteen invitees from my training class found each other on the Internet and became active on a LISTSERV. As we began to introduce ourselves, I came out. When we met in person at staging, word spread about me to the rest of the group.

From the time I met them I was very much at ease with the young adults who predominated my training group. I hadn't spent as much time with twenty-year-olds since I had been one myself. These kids lived in a social environment that was markedly different from that of the early 1970's when I was their age. They all knew gay characters on television and in movies; they have lesbian sisters and gay brothers;

they attended colleges with active gay student unions. For most of them, my being gay was a very big No Big Deal.

Our lengthy training before service as Volunteers included a wealth of information about local culture. We learned that public displays of affection in Mauritania are discouraged between women and men, but are perfectly acceptable between men and between women. Once we finally arrived in the country, I began to notice the common sight of men draped around one another as they sat in chairs or lay on mats in front of stores or homes. We learned that this, of course, does not necessarily signal their sexuality. One of my favorite sights remains that of two soldiers, uniformed, walking down the street holding hands. An army of lovers cannot fail!

It was a good thing that my fellow trainees knew about me, because it was from one of them that I had the occasion to meet Mamadou, my first gay Mauritanian. Mamadou had met Carl, another Peace Corps Volunteer, near the Senegal River in Kaédi, our training city. He invited Carl to his family's house for tea several times. Eventually, Mamadou told him, *"Je suis bisexuel."* Carl took it in stride, probably fortified after his having lived for ten years in San Francisco himself, and didn't unravel. All he needed to say was, *"Je ne suis pas comme ça."* And then, of course, Carl told me what had happened.

I persuaded him to introduce me to Mamadou, which happened just a few hours before we were sworn in as Peace Corps Volunteers. It was a fortunate coincidence that Mamadou was there in Kaédi to begin with. He was visiting family, but he really lived in Nouakchott, the capital, where I was going to be living.

Once Mamadou found out where I lived, there was no holding him back. Not only did he come to visit without notice, as is the custom here, but he usually brought a friend. This built up the network of gay men I met. It was not only a good way to meet other men, but just about the only one available to me, as there is no such thing as a gay bar or cruising area for making contacts.

Mamadou's introductions stopped during Ramadan, the Islamic holy month of fasting and avoiding temptation. But once that was over, he resumed bringing over several other men. Their ages ranged from their twenties to their forties and included both single and married guys. One evening he brought a man named Babah to my house for a visit. Babah was a smiling twenty-three-year-old who didn't say much. As usual, Mamadou was proud of himself, like a cat that brought a dead mouse home to his master. After a while, Mamadou employed one of his usual tactics: excusing himself from the room so that he could pray. Ostensibly, this was to give me an opportunity to get to know Babah better. He came back to find me and Babah talking. They had their soft drinks, we talked for a while longer, and then they left.

A few days later, when I was coming home from teaching an early evening class, I found Babah waiting for me on the small bench outside my apartment building. I did what was culturally expected of me to do here: I invited him in. We talked, touched, and cuddled. It was very enjoyable. A few days later, he was back. Then, the following week, he brought his friend Ismail.

The visit with Ismail came at a time when Molly, another Peace Corps Volunteer, was visiting me from the small and remote village where she had been living and working. Babah and Ismail were enchanted by her, and the next day, they came back to visit. Ismail proclaimed his love for her. Babah had a perpetually goony smile that let her know he liked her, too. Meanwhile, Molly and I were bemused as we shared our secret: these guys were falling in lust with our group's only out lesbian!

I was both touched and confused to see that they had brought Molly gifts and attached little love notes to them. It didn't bother me that they were showing their interest, but it did make me wonder about how they saw their own sexuality. It was my first indication that people elsewhere in the world are living and dealing with a more fluid definition of sexuality than the one we experience in the United States.

Babah and Ismail had done something that was out of the ordinary for most Mauritanians: they had rented a room in a house away from their own families. This gave them a degree of autonomy that most of their countrymen do not have at their age. During the next few weeks, the two of them continued to visit me—sometimes with social intent and sometimes sexual. I also invited them to a few dinners when other Volunteers were in town. They always picked out a favorite woman and let us know that they would be delighted if she could come and visit them in their room, which was about a mile away. The intent of their invitations was always clear to the women, and nobody ever took them up on their offer.

An athlete and avid soccer player, Babah was limber with a well-defined musculature. His behavior when women were present was always much different from when it was just all of us as men alone. He showed off his agility by stretching and doing other floor exercises, checking occasionally to see if the women were watching him, and then smiling at them if they made eye contact. And even though it was culturally acceptable for him to touch me in their presence, he would not do that. He only held my hand, leaned against me, or showed other affection when there were no women present.

In time, Babah told me about the woman he had wanted to marry, but whose family refused him permission because he was too poor. I asked him if he was looking for a wife. He said, "I have to tell you the truth. I love women. I will get married and have children, but my heart will always be for you."

Babah is clearly standing at a crossroads: the place where Societal Avenue bisects Inner Drive. And evidently he can pull this off—for the time being, at least, by getting some affection from a man, while operating with the expectations that this will not manifest into his entire future.

It played well with my circumstances, while I lived in Mauritania, but that did not mean that I didn't bring my own ambivalence to the situation. On the one hand, I had never entered into any relationship with the attitude that "he is fine for the time being." We both knew that I was there temporarily, so whatever it was that we had between us would come to an end in about a year. On the other hand, he was pleasant, kind, appreciative, and honest, which made it easy to help him out in any way I could.

Babah started working at a place near my house. One morning, while I was cooking oatmeal for breakfast, I gazed out the window and saw him walking by. I impulsively called to him and he came upstairs to join me for breakfast. That became a six-day-a-week ritual.

He started to come by about half an hour before he was due at work, eat his breakfast, take a shower, and then go to work with a lunch that I packed for him because he could not afford to buy anything on the low wages he was earning.

Whereas Ismail never invited me to meet or visit with his family, Babah did. I went to the house a few times, and was always treated as an honored guest. I don't know how he explained meeting me, but his family was pleasant and welcoming.

One morning, I got a call from Babah to tell me that his father had just died. Customary Muslim practices are similar to Jewish ones in that the deceased is buried as soon as possible and people visit the family home during the three days following the death. One local variation, however, is that mourning and visiting at home are done in rooms that are segregated by sex. For a short time, Babah and I sat alone in a small room. He held my hand and cried, but pulled himself together and put some space between us when other men entered the room.

His morning visits continued for about four months. One day he asked me if I would help him to get a visa so that he could go with me when I return to the United States. He did not understand the process that it takes to get a tourist visa. I tried to explain that it was a very complicated matter. Anyone wanting to visit the United States from Mauritania has to demonstrate quite clearly that they have compelling interests that will bring them back to their home country, that they will not represent a "flight risk" and stay in the United States.

Babah seemed to think otherwise. He insisted that all he needed was a letter from me, addressed to the U.S. Embassy, explaining that I would house him when he visits. As each of us defended our own understanding of the circumstances, Babah interpreted my explanation as a rejection, and his visits ceased for about two weeks.

He stopped by one evening after work to say that he had been upset with me, but that I probably didn't know why. Yes, it was about not being able to support his application for a visa. He had wanted to come and live with me, but I was rejecting him. I explained that I understood his feelings of being let down.

After yet another week, his demeanor showed a pronounced change when he came by one evening after work to tell me that the daughter of the owner of the business where he worked had taken a liking to him, and that he liked her, too. He seemed to be headed down the road that his culture has demarcated for him, and was not very troubled by having taken the detour to be with me. There was, of course, no way of knowing how the situation with me would have played out if I had decided to support his request by helping him to get a visa to visit the United States.

In addition to "Mamadou's men," there were others I met on my own during the course of living there. The unifying factor is that they were Muslims living in an Islamic republic. The way they make their way in the world reflects the society in which they were born, raised, and are currently living.

Early on in my stay, there was the taxi driver who first smiled at me for a little too long, giving me pause for concern that he wasn't keeping his eyes on the road, and then he put his hand in my lap. He expressed an interest in getting together, but it could not be in his place because he lived with his wife, children, and extended family. There was also the hotel manager who offered to show me more than a room, then explained that he was engaged to be married to a woman who already has children.

One business owner, upon finding out I was an American, told me that the best part about the visit to his brother in "Texas, Dallas" was that he could see "sexy movies" at video arcades. In his shop, he displayed a photo of his two adorable children. His family lived in a different Muslim country, which left him fairly independent and allowed us to become friends. I met a kickboxing instructor on public transportation when he was going with his wife to a clinic. He made sure to tell me that he gives massage at the sports center where he works, and he showed me where it was on a map, and made sure that I had his phone number so I could arrange my appointment.

These men represented a cross-section of the ethnicities that live in Mauritania. Some are Moors, the descendents of Arabs and Berbers who give the country its Middle-Eastern flavor, and some are Pulaar,

Soninke, and Wolof, whose heritages reflect their black sub-Saharan roots.

I have heard people say, "We don't have homosexuals in Mauritania." Most Americans laugh at what they perceive to be such a naïve and absurd statement. After all, we know about the distribution of gay people in our own culture, and we conclude that there is a worldwide population of a given percentage of "homosexuals" in every society. But I have come to understand that the statement "We don't have homosexuals in Mauritania" means something else altogether to the people who say it. Western television and movies are widely available and watched here. Via these media, Mauritanians see American and European gay people demonstrating in the streets for their equality, petitioning their governments for the right to marry, leaving their extended families, and setting up house together so they can live independently as a couple. That is what "being gay" looks like to people there. When homosexuality is portrayed in those terms, the Mauritanians are right—they don't have (those kind of) gay people here! By contrast, men having sex with men—a critical part of the Western definition for being gay—well, that is something totally different!

The family is the foundation and building block of the Mauritanian society. It is not only the closest thing to a social security administration in the institutional sense, but also is the bedrock of the administration of each individual's social security. It's the family that takes care of you, no matter the circumstances—sick, handicapped, old, *n'importe quoi.* It's almost unheard of to cut family ties because one is different, to come out as being gay and then leave the bosom of the family to live either alone or with another person.

It is instructive to understand the translation from the Arabic of the first question people ask when they meet: "Who are you from?" Note that they are not asking *where,* which would be just the name of a village or town, but *who.* People's identity and sense of solidarity stems from the tribe, the family, the home. They take great pride in these connections. It would be antithetical to demonstrate in the streets in order to shine a light on the fact that they belong to a different class of people. Doing so would alienate them from the people on whom they are most dependent.

In Mauritania, respect for and obligations to family members increase with age. Many people have asked me if it is true that Americans provide separate housing for our older relatives, away from our families. The idea of taking a loved one and putting him or her in such a place is disrespectful and shameful. Although young people here have their own music, as in Western societies, when it comes to worshipping of youth, as it exists in the United States, there is nothing comparable. Youth are not taken seriously. I remarked to a twenty-seven-year-old friend that it would be very unusual in my country for me to be hanging out with somebody his age. His spontaneous reply was sincere, respectful, and touching: "What I'm going to learn from you, I'm not going to learn from anyone my age."

Everyone is expected to marry and raise children. Familial respect comes not only with age, but from adhering to cultural expectations. Children sincerely do not want to disappoint their family. One's actions, including choice of marriage partner, involve the entire family. This is a communal society in which a person does not head out into the world on his or her own, nor does he or she ignore the imperatives of the elders. Placing your relatives in the care of others, following your dreams, pursuing your goals, reaching your potential, carrying on a private life in which one comes and goes freely and unquestioned, demonstrating for the rights of an amorphous and unknown minority group—these are all Western concepts that do not apply to Mauritania. This is partly due to the cultural, religious, and intellectual conditions, but considerable attention needs to be paid to the stark financial reality that most people are preoccupied with the daily struggle of making ends meet in this poverty-stricken land.

As I pause to figure out the local social landscape and the way that gay people fit in, it helps to add my observation that the typical Mauritanian has a healthy disrespect for anything that is "official," which apparently includes his or her own religious doctrines. He or she picks and chooses judiciously among the offerings of the Western cultural smorgasbord as he or she says yes to cars, but no to seat belts and other rules of the road; yes to movies and television, but no to books; yes to Coca-Cola, but no to fruits and vegetables (particularly in the Moors' diet); yes to post offices, but no to home delivery; yes to

streets, but no to house numbers and street names. This may be a result of the prevailing (though declining) nomadic heritage and its way
of life, which celebrates a high degree of self-sufficiency. I think of it as
desert machismo.

The Islam practiced in Mauritania is tolerant and gentle. Though
consumption of alcohol is "officially" prohibited and not easy to find,
Mauritanians do consume it. Although many people I know do not
drink, citing religious principles, they concede that others have the
right to do so if they want to, as long as they do not get drunk in public. Furthermore, I have never heard a nondrinker take a superior tone
with respect to this issue.

Likewise, I know dozens of people who do not fast during the day-
light hours of Ramadan—some of whom flout convention and eat in
restaurants! For every person who answers the calls of the muezzin by
going to the mosque or finding another public place in which to pray,
there are many who have told me that they "just don't do that,"
avoiding the proscribed five-times-a-day schedule of prayer.

The "official" perspective is that homosexuals can be put to death,
but this has never happened in Mauritania. People who act out as homosexuals appear to be tolerated with the same laissez-faire attitude
accorded to other aspects of the society. "We are a peaceful country,"
many Mauritanians have told me. When one of my adult students invited me to his home, we watched a televised report from Spain, in
which there was a demonstration about gay people being allowed to
marry. Selme, my student, turned to me unsolicited and said, "If I had
a gay brother, I would have to accept him. He is my family. And I
could not let anyone say anything against him because he is my
brother and I would have to protect him."

Similarly, my students in the teacher trainee program one day held
a discussion in which they concluded that they did not have a problem
accepting gay people. More emotionally charged for them was the issue about married men being able to spend more time with their male
friends than with their wives. Despite these young people unwittingly
expressing their support for my sexuality, my working with them was
in an official Peace Corps capacity—not as a gay crusader—and I
never did come out to them.

Drawing definitive conclusions about a society after living there for a little more than a year is not a wise, safe, or responsible action on my part. If a society's culture is a mosaic of thousands of little tiles, then I like to think that what I have been able to piece together has been a tableau in which certain aspects have become discernable, some are a little less clear, and others remain in a way that I will never see as whole and comprehensible. Living there as a temporary resident in such a different world is something with which I must make not only my own sense but my own sense of peace.

# ஃ 2          I Want Your Eyes

*David Stevens*

Determined to go to bed early for once.

I lie under my wheezy fan, lights firmly out. But my heart pounds, my mind whirs. Skin seeks comfort in cool cotton sheets, but any respite is momentary.

I am aware of sounds intruding into the room. A distant pulse of Hindi movie music escaping some sweaty slave quarters. A snatch of Malayalam—or is that Tamil? The yapping of wild dogs, mongrels running down from the hills for their nightly forage in garbage bins at the edge of town.

Yes, Muttrah at night is a restless and relentlessly noisy place. Arab cities come alive at the sunset prayer and this corner of Muscat, capital of The Sultanate of Oman, is no exception.

I roll over, but a new, much closer sound comes to me. Distantly at first, then steadily increasing in volume. The shocking thump of ball against tile, a tricycle scooting along a protesting floor. Children. Even though it's close to midnight and school starts at 7:30 a.m., still they play on in the corridors of my building.

The prospect of sleep evaporates. A late-night walk seems the best strategy.

I walk to the window and pull back the beach towel that serves as a curtain. A tangle of low buildings, minarets, and twisted lanes bathe under a perfect crescent moon.

I drift toward the bathroom mirror. It has been fixed low on the wall so that I have to bend my knees to see my face. Blue eyes stare back at me, blinking bright over purplish bags. My features are sharp and pale under a fluorescent glow. Short, fair hair that comes to life with the caress of a brush. I throw water on my dry skin.

*Gay Travels in the Muslim World*
© 2007 by The Haworth Press, Inc. All rights reserved.
doi:10.1300/5481_02

I walk to the wardrobe. Familiar faces stare from photos tacked on to the doors. One short, dark boy stands out from the collage. The boy at the seaside, the boy by a stand of trees, the boy in a café. I avert my gaze from his recurring image as I slap on a T-shirt and jeans. Nothing too fancy. Sneakers slipped on at the door. No money or other accessories needed. The night calls for nothing but me.

I leave my apartment. The noisy children have vanished, leaving a single child's shoe outside my door as a memento of their visit.

I descend to ground level. A clammy tendril of air wafts up the stairway to greet me. Outside it is no cooler—a bath laced with sea salt and sweat.

I enter the alley running between my block and the Shia mosque next door. I catch sight of an emaciated tail withdrawing into the shadows of a broken doorway. A cat? I look again but the shadows are empty.

At the far end of the alley, an Indian man is hurrying my way. He noisily clears his throat and spits. I hear the thud as his phlegm hits the tired ground.

"Good evening, sir," he says as he passes.

His face is in shadow. I wonder if I should recognize him.

Phantom cats and spittle. I am glad to leave this sordid space.

I pause at the busy road separating me from the black and silver harbor. Orange-and-white striped taxis honk at me, touting for business. I ignore them, waiting for a break in the traffic.

Reaching the other side, I stop for a minute, taking in a view that never fails to thrill. The Sultan's ships glisten from their safe berths across the harbor, the bright and busy port, the jagged hills careering down to meet the sea.

The high tide laps politely at the corniche walls. I look down and momentarily lose myself in the transparent sea. Muttrah Fort perches on a rocky headland above the the corniche footpath, its ochre walls hanging ghostlike above the heads of late night pedestrians. My pace quickens as I make my way toward it.

Every fifteen yards or so along my path are luridly colored bas-reliefs of local bird life. I scarcely glance at them now, but remember a time when I would strain to match their image to the long-necked birds I would see striding along the shoreline.

I walk the walk, look the look. The footpath is crowded with a thousand eyes and all of them are looking at me. I pass by Arabs, Indians, Pakistanis—all men and all drawn to this place in search of something. Is it the thrill of a cool breeze playing on their face or the prospect of something different at which to look? As we pass each other we exchange glances, our cultures lapping at each other like the waves in the harbor.

The Pakistani navy is in town. Groups of disoriented sailors with blizzard white uniforms and gaudy shopping bags move in tight bunches up and down the corniche. Several of them hold hands. Yet this is not a Western style of holding hands, it is something altogether lighter, less possessive, with fingers barely touching.

I pass several bus-stop-like shelters housing clumps of men, firmly segregated by race. I recognize some of them as regulars who bring strips of carpet to sit on and thermoses of coffee to drink while they chat and gaze out to sea.

I casually eye the groups, more out of habit than anything else. They eye me back. How do I appear to them, this outsider invading their territory? Their eyes give me no clues. I see empty eyes, sad eyes, occasionally hostile eyes. Do they stare at me because I am different or do they gaze with desire? And if so, is it for my culture or my body?

Men by themselves are rare. I pass a handsome Omani man sitting on the corniche wall with a cigarette between his long brown fingers. He wears his colorful *cuma,* an Omani cap, at a jaunty angle and his mustard-colored dishdasha has risen up to reveal tantalizingly hairy calves. I note the carefully made holes in his ears—not in his earlobes but deep inside the cartilages—a pre-Islamic custom still practiced on some male babies to ward off evil spirits. I decide it suits him.

The man sees me studying him and smiles. Our eyes meet and part company in the kiss of a second. I note his location before continuing on my way.

Farther on, a school of Indian fishermen try their luck with single lines and pieces of white bread. This basic apparatus appears to work well as they bring in a constant stream of small, gasping fish. Once caught, the fish are entombed in black plastic bags. The bags rest on the footpath, twitching in time to their occupant's death throes.

Bypassing this casual carnage, I come across an arresting sight. A young guy sitting alone listening to a Walkman. With his dark, curly hair, carefully shaped goatee beard—or "French" as they call them here—and Euro uniform of baggy jeans and shiny football shirt, he looks more Italian than Arabic, though the burnt olive color of his skin suggests Sicily, not Tuscany.

I continue on but then, a little way off, stop for another look. As casually as I can, I focus on the waters of Muttrah Harbor before glancing back to where he's slouching on his solitary bench. Eyes that have been following me are quickly diverted. Yes, I've been noticed.

I perch on the harbor wall about ten yards from him. Concentrate on the view while thinking about strategy.

Minutes pass and I grow impatient. Taking a chance, I walk back past him and occupy an empty bench about three yards from his. He doesn't look at me as I pass but I seize the opportunity to study him up close. I note the angry scar on one side of his forehead and a slight crook at the end of his long, thin nose. This boy's a fighter.

I sit on my seat while he remains on his. He appears oblivious to my presence, staring straight ahead toward the sea. Occasionally he taps a foot in time to some unknown beat. A woman without a face floats past us.

After several minutes, I grow tired of this game and launch myself once again onto the footpath, beginning to promenade past him once more. However, this time, as soon as I get close, he removes his headphones and our eyes meet.

"*K'aif falak?*" How are you? I ask. My Arabic sounds stilted in the dead night air.

"*Tamam.*" He is well.

His voice is a little higher than I imagined it would be, his brown eyes stoned on something illicit.

"*Kallum Inglese?*" I ask if he understands my language.

"*Swaya Inglese.*" A little. He says it almost as a challenge.

I sit down next to him and he responds by moving a little to accommodate me. I take a deep breath, summoning up my reserves of small talk in his tongue—this untamable language that surrounds me.

Our conversation proceeds haltingly, with me asking all the questions. His name is Ahmed Al Balushi and he's a local. He lives with his family around the corner.

*"Fi shugal?"* I ask if he has work.

He does but I have some trouble understanding what it is. I glance down at his hands as he tries to describe his job. They are large and chafed red. Between the thumb and the forefinger on his right hand is a small tattoo. It is a symbol with Arabic letters next to it. It looks homemade and somehow scares me.

I still can't understand exactly what his job entails—something to do with cars—and silence overtakes us. From my side there are no more questions to ask except the obvious one. A wave of exhaustion flows over me. It is very late at night to play such games with this stoned boy.

Time to go.

*"Yalla,"* I say, shifting to face him.

*"Bin sur bait com?"* You go to your home. It is a statement rather than a question.

I nod in agreement and meet his hazy brown eyes, searching for something to say he might like to join me. Nothing is there.

*"In zain."* Okay. His fingers are already straying back to his Walkman, ready to reactivate it.

*"Maa'salaama."* I stand up, offering my hand for him to shake. When his comes it is warm and soft. I imagine this hand on my body and shiver with desire. He leaves his hand in mine for a moment too long.

I take a final look at my late-night companion. I notice a mischievous sparkle has come into his eyes. They dive into my own. Deeply. Possessively. Jealously.

"I want your eyes." The words are spoken in perfect English.

I'm not sure how to respond, so I say nothing.

His hand finally releases mine. I leave him on his bench, heading back the way I have come.

An image comes to me. I imagine my eyes, deftly plucked from their sockets and left lying on the corniche footpath, like a discarded fish carcass. I shudder and quicken my pace.

I feel my friend's eyes boring into my back and neck but don't turn around. My eyes are safer focused firmly ahead.

# A Market and a Mosque

*Martin Foreman*

Sylhet, Bangladesh: It's eight o'clock in the evening and Tarique and Paritosh are taking me out to look at the cruising spots. Until I flew in here this afternoon, all I knew of this provincial city and the surrounding area was that it was where most of the Bangladeshis in the UK come from—and since most of the Bangladeshis in the UK live in my home borough of Tower Hamlets, I feel a kind of affinity with the place. Whether or not Sylhet feels an affinity with me is a different matter.

We walk out of the Holy Side Hotel into the evening heat. I've been living in a tropical climate for half a year now and I am still disappointed by having to wear clothes when I go out. Despite that most human bodies are better covered than bared, I'm a firm proponent of minimum clothing (loincloths for both sexes and a comfortable bra for women) any time the temperature rises above twenty degrees. Anyhow, I put that thought behind me as we walk toward the main road and Paritosh stops a baby taxi—one of the motor-powered three-wheelers ubiquitous in South and Southeast Asia—and negotiates a ride.

Or rather fails to negotiate it. The driver has seen the presence of a white man and insists that Paritosh pay one hundred taka, almost two dollars, to take us the ten-minute ride to the market. Paritosh, annoyed, waves him away and stops the next baby taxi. His price is fifty taka, still higher than market rate, but within reason. The three of us clamber in and head off.

Paritosh works for the Bandhu Social Welfare Society, a national organization that provides information on HIV and other issues for men who have sex with men. He's the last stop on my five-day fact-

*Gay Travels in the Muslim World*
© 2007 by The Haworth Press, Inc. All rights reserved.
doi:10.1300/5481_03

finding visit, undertaken as part of a commission to see what additional information my health organization needs on sex between men. For four days I've been talking with various experts about every aspect of the subject, from indigenous identities to changing patterns of sexual behavior. It's been a fascinating time, learning people's different perspectives on the subject and putting them together in a coherent framework. I'm not the first person to do this by any means—Shivananda Khan is a walking encyclopedia on the subject—but like the sparrow perched on the back of an eagle, I'm vain enough to think that I can push our knowledge just a little bit further.

We drive through streets crowded with pedestrians, rickshaws, baby taxis, and the occasional car, getting off at the edge of the market, where Paritosh negotiates with the driver to stay until we return. We're in a crowded street with little lighting, and the faces that we pass look at me as if not quite certain what they've seen. After a hundred yards or so, when the street widens into an irregularly shaped square where open shops cast their light on traders whose wares are displayed on mats on the street in front of them, we step back into the shade of a deserted building and watch the scene.

Sylhet is known as the most conservative and religious part of Muslim Bangladesh. This explains why so few women are in the street, although those women who can be seen are not veiled and some do not even wear scarves. Still, this is an almost exclusively male population, of all ages and sizes, passing by on foot, rickshaw, or baby taxi, or waiting for customers. This is a well-known cruising spot, I have been told, and for a few minutes I see nothing that tells me that any of these men is seeking sex. Then, at the same time Tarique points him out to me, I see a slender youth standing almost motionless as others walk past him, the moment presenting itself in a cinematic special effect in which his movements are slowed while everyone else's have sped up.

And there's another and another and another. Dotted around me are elegant, handsome young men in shirts and lunghi—long skirts—that are a little more colorful, a little more clean, and a little more tightly bound than the men around them. They are staring into the distance with an expression that is at once distant and focused, as if announcing that they have no business here. But business they do have, because from time to time, someone will approach. When they do, the ritual seems to be that neither addresses the other immediately, but instead stares past as if it were coincidence that they were so close, then, almost without looking at each other, a desultory conversation begins.

And so an old man in white with a thick moustache and a curved back approaches the haughtiest youth, a fair-skinned, broad-faced young man who in other circumstances might have a career as an actor or a model, but the conversation does not go far. A few minutes later I see the old man in another part of the market drinking a tea with another youth. They are more engaged, and in a few minutes they will disappear down an alleyway to where a room can be rented for fifty taka, or less than a dollar, for an hour.

We are joined by Ajoy, a Bandhu peer educator, who each evening goes out and talks to young men and tells them about HIV/AIDS and condoms and the drop-in center where they can see a doctor and meet other young men like themselves. I've already spoken to men who sell sex in Dhaka. I would like to do so here in Sylhet, but I do not want to deprive them of their earning time and I do not want to be the center of attraction.

Things are changing, Ajoy tells me, in a number of ways. First, the money that the men make is going up—fifty to one hundred taka now, instead of thirty to fifty taka two or three years ago. This means that their overall income can now be between 10,000 and 15,000 taka a month—considerably more than Ajoy or Paritosh make. It's down to the fact that the town and its surroundings may appear as poor as elsewhere in Bangladesh, but the UK connection, with money sent home regularly or with emigrants returning to visit their families, means that more money is around waiting to be spent. But many, it seems, spend as quickly as they earn, and the idea of saving, of training for a job for when they are over twenty-five or thirty years of age and no longer able to count on their looks, does not occur to them.

And the second change? More condom use. Good news in a country where sex between men is widespread but HIV rates are still very low. What doesn't seem to be happening, unlike in Dhaka, is a change to oral sex. There, my informants tell me, clients increasingly want to avoid the risk of contracting HIV in anal sex, and, I assume, they are also increasingly enjoying the pleasures of mouthwork. Sex workers in Dhaka are pleased too, partly because it is safer and easier and partly because they can charge more money. But in Sylhet another change is taking place—clients are increasingly taking the passive role and the effeminate young men are taking on an unaccustomed masculine role.

I suspect that exterior forces are at work here. In Thailand the rigid division between "gay king" and "gay queen" is breaking down as imported pornography shows that masculine men enjoy being fucked as much as any effeminate queen. And, as expected, sex movies and images are easily available in Sylhet. Paritosh points out a stall where DVDs showing men and women, men and men and, no doubt women and women can be bought.

It's time to move on. We walk back into the dark crowd. Many people seem unaware of me, but I am conscious of the glances of those who see me and stare directly into my eyes with an expression that melds curiosity with—I wonder if I am being irrational—hostility. I do not feel unsafe, despite that this is a violent country where street brawls over the pettiest of excuses are common, where the drivers of baby taxis in Dhaka lock themselves in metal cages to protect themselves from rioting mobs, and where the two leading political parties sponsor gangs of competing thugs.

It is a short ride to the Shahjalal Mazar, the shrine in which centuries ago a Bengali saint died. We go through an archway and find ourselves in a marble courtyard outside a tall, white mosque that stands impressively against the dark blue night. Directly in front of us are a tall, broad-shouldered young man and his equally impressive girlfriend or bride. He is in casual clothes and she, unveiled, in a handsome, dark red sari. But no other women are there, and many of the men are wearing the white caps that denote dedicated believers. I look around; as in the market, people seem to be moving with a sense of purpose, even if it is only two or three gathered in conversation, and I see no "sensitive" young men loitering ostensibly to take the evening air. Yet this location is a well-known place for religious men to find young friends. After all, sex between men in Bangladesh may be widespread, but it is unacknowledged—two men can be together, hold hands, even sleep in the same bed without others construing a sexual relationship. Men who are quick to preserve the chastity and fidelity of women turn to other men to slake their lust.

In the middle of the square I feel exposed. There is more light here, and already more eyes are turning on me than did in the market. We walk toward a pool in which earlier in the year the fish that lived there were poisoned, at about the time a bomb exploded nearby, killing two people. Paritosh points out two young men squatting by the pool, deep in conversation, one of his peer educators and a sex worker. I look around to see if I can spot other men for sale and find my eyes crossing with a short, middle-aged man in a yellow shirt and tie who asks me, in excellent, if accented, English, and in a tone that is nearer hostile than friendly, where I am from. I tell him, and the idea that Sylhetis might feel an affinity with Londoners evaporates in the intensity of his gaze.

"Why are you here?" he asks. I give him an answer that is almost true—to see this place, because I had heard it commemorates a famous martyr.

"Why do you like it?" he asks. I hadn't told him I liked it, and had not developed an opinion. My answer is poor, only that the shrine is impressive and white. Within the space of this brief conversation we have been surrounded by at least twenty others, all male, from plump pubescent boys to skinny middle-aged men. Not one smiles in welcome. My inquisitor repeats the question, but I have already turned away from him to suggest, to Paritosh's and Tarique's obvious relief, that maybe we should move on. I smile weakly at the man in yellow and follow my guides down a path that seems to lead nowhere in particular. For the first few paces my shoulders are tense, but we are not being followed.

We are indeed going nowhere in particular. If my curiosity is satisfied, Paritosh and Tarique imply, they can take me back to the hotel. Part of me wants to stay out, to observe the scene a little more, to see one of the older religious men approach a younger man, to watch them negotiate and walk away together, but it's impossible; to stand still would be to attract another inquisitive crowd. As we head back across the square, the lights suddenly go out. Without saying a word, Paritosh's hands meet and hold on to mine (given his good looks and welcoming personality, it's a gesture I would have preferred at another time). Tarique quickly does the same, and the three of us walk at a resolute pace back into secular streets.

I spend the rest of the evening watching cable television and marveling at the homoerotic advertisements on the Star network aimed at India—in particular the hips of the handsome youth modeling "Killer—revealingly low jeans," and the assortment of young men sporting Try International underwear. The next day, Tarique and I spend four hours at the airport, the victims of a flight cancelled thanks to a long, impressive, and blinding downpour. I spend some of the time watching a Hindi karate film that is refreshingly free of the song and dance that interrupts most Bollywood films.

The next day, I am back home, and I read on BBC's Web site that a bomb has exploded at the mosque in attempt to kill the new British High Commissioner, the diplomatic representative for the Queen, and a man who was himself born in Sylhet. It is clear that for some Sylhetis at least, the bonds that tie their homeland with Britain are bonds not of love, but of hate.

# Adventures in Afghanistan
*Michael Luongo*

"I knew what you wanted when you told me I was attractive. I am from Kabul, I know these things," Munir said with a sophisticated, almost jaded, air as he put his jacket back on, part of a neat, though frayed and dusty, black suit. Even amid rubble, he tried hard to keep a sense of money and fashion about him. Indeed, he was almost foppish, representing a side of Kabul few foreigners know of. In spite of its post-war ruin and poverty, this is a capital city, cosmopolitan in outlook, with, at times, an anything-goes, Casablanca-esque atmosphere.

However, this cute, twenty-one-year-old English teacher told me I was too old for him. I was thirty-five at the time and not much used to ageism, but in a country where few men hit their midforties, his statment wasn't hard to fathom.

We met on the city's dusty streets, just in front of the Ministry of the Interior building. I was on my way to a crafts shop, and as we passed, he held my stare and threw glances back my way. It could have been Santa Monica Boulevard. Half an hour flew by as we conversed, men in uniform holding guns and women in burkas parading back and forth as I expounded on his looks and said I wanted to know him better. He kept telling me his father was a policeman, bringing an interesting edge to my flirtation. Was he telling me this to make me stop or to say he had special privileges?

Like others I met in Kabul and told I was gay, Munir insisted I should have gone to Kandahar—reputed to be Afghanistan's gay capital—where he said "men like men." Ironically, the Taliban's headquarters had been in that very city. Yes, they did murder gay men, famously toppling walls over them, but eventually some came to like what they saw. If Jerry Falwell had churches only in West Hollywood

doi:10.1300/5481_04

from which to spew his rhetoric and gain parishioners, he'd have to tolerate, and absorb, much of behavior he claimed to be against.

Though I couldn't have Munir, he was sure his twenty-six-year-old friend, already partnered with a thirty-five-year-old man, would like to meet me. After all, Munir said, "This is Kabul. Anything can be arranged." We made plans to meet later at his house. I did not know yet, but through Munir, I would become privy to a group of Kabul men, some soldiers, who threw parties with the chance of sex between men.

Although my interaction with Munir was clear-cut, other encounters ranged from vaguely subtle to outlandishly open. On first glance, so many men hold hands in Kabul you'd swear you were in Chelsea. But if you're familiar with Islamic countries, this means nothing. However, under the surface, there's more going on in this dusty, crumbled capital. My most interesting meetings were without my translator when it was just me, unfiltered, alone with Afghan men.

Remember the Impulse body spray commercials from years ago? Walking in Kabul is like living in one. A few times on Flower Street, named for its florists and wedding shops, men offered bouquets and said they loved me, the kind of greeting Bush hoped American soldiers would have in Baghdad after that ill-fated invasion. In America, though, no man ever greets me spontaneously like this, and if they did, I'd think they're psycho, but here in Kabul the offers of love and flowers out of the blue were endearing. Still, like holding hands, this didn't always mean anything.

Yet one experience with a young florist clearly meant more. I'd been wandering a remote street, photographing workers and children for nearly an hour. The florist watched me with shy curiosity. When I photographed him, I told him he was very handsome, saying it in a way that my deeper intentions were obvious. He invited me into the shop, showing me various wedding arrangements.

He had no girlfriend and wanted no wife. He became sad when I asked if he liked other men.

"People in Afghanistan are very shy," he said. He turned away and let me hold his hand, my fingers rubbing against his palm. Even though heavy foot traffic passed outside, it seemed not to matter. It was only when I asked to kiss him that he worried, looking into my eyes with a nervous smile.

He gave me a vase of plastic flowers and then said some words in Dari, the Afghan language, explaining, "That means I love you." I grabbed his hand again, kissing him on the cheeks, close to his lips. At that moment, his friend walked in, nearly laughing. I hoped it was simply at me, the crazy gay foreigner, and that my indiscretions were no harm. (I visited again and all was fine.) I left, heading downtown past the city's few tall buildings and the yellow Shah do Shamshira mosque on my way back to my hotel, the vase of flowers colorfully poking from my backpack.

This was life on the street, but one Afghan national who worked in an embassy gave me a more official overview of what we in the West would call gay aspects of Afghan culture. He did not want to be identified, preferring to use only his first name, Mohammed, which of course is nearly everyone's first name. Certain Afghan ethnic groups, he explained, especially the Uzbeks and Pashtuns, were particularly known for male interactions. Like Munir before, he too said the city with the greatest reputation for man-on-man love was Kandahar. According to Mohammed, "they were even holding wedding ceremonies after the Taliban arrived." The Taliban tried to control it, he explained, but "it was so common in Kandahar, they were able to embrace it. Even during the Taliban, it was clearly visible. Commanders had boys."

Many relationships bordered on pedophilia, however, and Mohammed's father never took him to Kandahar as a teenager, largely because he worried people would see them holding hands and assume they were lovers.

From ancient times, other homosexual aspects existed in Afghanistan. This still continues according to Mohammed at rural weddings outside of the northern city of Mazar-i-Sharif, where dancer-boys entertain all-male crowds, wearing anklets that make music as they move. Sometimes, he explained, they "dress him like a woman." Many of the boys are available for sex, too.

"It has two parts—the dancing part and the sexual part. The sexual part, no one will confess."

Yet while these relationships are known, they are not always discussed openly. They are illegal too, in spite of their prevalence.

"The sexual part, it's a problem. The man and the boy can go to jail." I eventually went to Mazar-i-Sharif on a later visit and found the drag-dancing videos on DVD, sold in shops all over town, but I was never sure if it equated to pornography or not.

Other areas in the country had some of these traditions. Afghan Americans I knew had told me similar stories, but never in such rich detail. They agreed too that many cases were pedophilia, one more of the horrible abuses in Afghanistan.

I wanted to go to Kandahar because of its gay reputation, but to find *grown* men. This existed, according to Mohammed, but he also explained that I'd get beaten up if I went snooping around. Based on that and other warnings, I skipped Kandahar on my first trip, though I was able to make it the next year, and was amazed by both the beauty of this holy city and its homoerotic wonders, the sensual and the sacred often side by side.

Still, as I wandered in the capital of Kabul, Kandahar's gay reputation came up with young Afghan men I photographed in the city's Babur Gardens pool, a modern amenity built by the Russians into a Mogul-era garden complex. Throughout my trip, the comfort Afghan men have with their bodies surprised me, even seminude in front of a camera. After the fall of the Taliban, many young men became obsessed with working out and polishing their image, a Kabul metrosexual movement, if you will. Such men, so proud of their bodies, would ask me to photograph them at pools, saunas, and gyms. At the pool, I questioned these men through my translator about body image under the Taliban. Tellingly, many laughed and said that although the Taliban banned being unclothed in public, they actually were made up of gay men from Kandahar, "playboys" as they called them using the English word, who loved to see naked men. It was treated as a joke, but that it simply came up in conversation is what struck me.

I had many reasons for coming to Afghanistan. After September 11, I was able to help in the cleanup of Ground Zero. Digging in the rubble of the Twin Towers for the dead bodies of my fellow New

Yorkers a few days after the tragedy, I swore I would see Afghanistan to better understand what had happened. As a New Yorker, I firmly believe that we are now forever linked to Kabul and must see the damage terrorism —both created by us as well as by other nations— does to the world in order to bring about peace. Unfortunately, few in Washington share that view.

Beyond this, from a gay perspective, I was constantly reading articles hinting at Afghan homosexuality. The *Scotsman,* in a lurid and homophobic article mentioned makeup-covered Afghan farmers who greeted British soldiers with offers of sex. *Details* magazine discussed it in the context of Islamic gender separation, along with a review of the book *Taliban,* a collection of effeminate warrior images found in Kandahar by a photographer named Thomas Dworzak. Various books by straight travelers mentioned it too, like Jason Elliot's *An Unexpected Light,* in which he discussed how Afghan men made passes at him because of his soft skin, undamaged by years of war and worry as was theirs. The only explicit, first-person reference appeared in the gay South-Asian magazine *Trikone* about a gay Afghan living in Pakistan. But to the best of my knowledge, no gay Westerner had infiltrated gay Afghan life to bring the story back to the rest of the world. I decided I would be the one to do this. Every Afghan American I knew worried, but once I was actually here, I realized Afghanistan was safer than the news would have you think. Still, how much of a risk was I willing to take for this story in one of the world's most conservative Muslim countries?

All this passed through my mind once it was time to meet Munir. I was staying at the Mustafa Hotel, full of journalists and odd characters, some here in Kabul for dubious reasons they would never quite disclose. The owner, an Afghan American from New Jersey, knew I was investigating Kabul's gay side, but I was not out to his staff. I simply told them I was doing interviews. The hotel's protective assistant manager feared Al-Qaeda insurgents and always wanted to know my whereabouts. I made him speak to my cab driver in Dari, the Afghan language, to clarify Munir's directions, but he thought the whole thing odd, constantly asking me why I was heading there. When my cab pulled away, he was left standing in the dust with a baffled look at my refusing to have the hotel's driver take me there and wait outside the address he kept telling me I should not go to in the first place.

Munir said he was only five minutes from downtown Kabul, but the cab ride seemed to last forever, and as we moved along we began slipping from the Kabul I recognized into places where electricity no longer worked. I called him on my rented cell phone, but he sounded drunk, and I could hear people laughing in the background. He'd invited friends to meet me, he said, which made me suspicious. Thinking we were lost, I handed the driver the phone. This only worried me more, though, because they engaged in a long conversation, the driver laughing and looking at me through the rearview mirror. What was he telling him? Was he purposely lost?

I was painfully curious what a gay party would be like in Kabul, but at the same time, I wondered if I were being led into a trap. I wanted a scoop, but I didn't want to be a gay Daniel Pearl.

After nearly a half hour of driving, we finally arrived, and Munir was on the darkened street with a few friends. One, named Syed, traditionally dressed in a long white robe, a skull cap, and beard, said that he was my intended. In broken but excited English, he mentioned his lover, whom he called "my handsome." Munir led us up the street and said he had a place for us, his "special room for men." A red light was shining from a second-floor window, and loud talking indicated the house was full. My first thought was that I had somehow been invited to a gay Afghan brothel. Munir opened a metal door and we walked into a dark passageway to an unlit, open-air staircase. Even as I worried what I was getting myself into, I stared in amazement at the clear Afghan sky, full of stars made all the brighter by the intensely dark, electricity-sparse Kabul evening.

When I entered the "special room" there were about eight men, most in their twenties and thirties, sprawled on cushions. All were shoeless, but in case I needed to bolt from the room, I kept my boots on, trailing dust along the brilliant red carpets. I sat self-consciously at the place of honor they motioned for me to take under a large window. Through a wall, I could hear women in the house, but I never saw any of them.

I felt on display, leered at, so many men around me. Soon more men entered, including Munir's father. One man could do nothing but stare, his eyes transfixed on me every time I looked his way, his face offering the same expression as terrorists stereotyped on television. If I were here to meet Syed, who were all these other men? The conversation was stilted, but I forced it through a talk-show-host smile, asking who knew English, making Munir translate when needed. Perhaps they needed to be put at ease as much as I did.

I asked about their lives under the Taliban, my favorite question on this first visit to Afghanistan no matter where I was, and one that fueled hours of conversation with strangers of all kinds. I wondered who wore beards then and asked if they kept pictures from the time, even though photographs were illegal under the Taliban's strict rules. This broke the tension, and out came several photo albums.

These were not men who sip cosmos and discuss *Queer Eye,* there was no doubt about their masculinity. Munir's brother Abdul was a martial-arts teacher for the Afghan army, Syed was an auto mechanic, and several were bodybuilders. Virtually all had fought against the Taliban. They proudly showed me pictures of themselves in the army, one valiantly parachuting out of helicopters. Each searched intensely for my reaction to his photos. It was as if each wanted to prove his bravery, to impress me, I felt, in the hopes I might choose him, though exactly for what I had no idea. Yet they were all obviously vying for my approval, and with each photo I felt as if I were being wooed, something, to be honest, no man had ever before tried to do to me before. Proving courage against the Taliban seemed to be their erotic calling card, the edge each tried to have over their competitors in the room surrounding me.

The desire to discuss sex soon became apparent. One young man asked about English slang words, offering that the Dari word for "milk" also means masturbation, making me think he wanted to start a circle-jerk. He then talked about prostitutes, mentioning a Chinese restaurant near my hotel that fronts for a brothel, clueing me in to the open secret that Kabul is rampant with prostitution, a curious fact few Westerners seem to believe when I tell them.

This young man was only twenty, and was married with children. I asked how in a traditionally Islamic country he knew of such things. He then challenged me, asking me about a wife or a girlfriend. I thought this was silly—he had to know I was gay. There suddenly arose laughs and comments from the group that Munir refused to translate. Finally, the young man said, "when we meet a man who does not have a wife, and does not have a girlfriend, we call him a sissy. What is another word for that in English?" I knew he was going for "gay," but instead I said that sissy can mean someone who is weak or afraid. I was here in Afghanistan, so I certainly could not fit such a definition, I told him. One of the men, Ali, a brutally handsome man with wildly wavy hair, then put his arm around me and nudged closer. He played with the muscles on my arms, comparing them to his own, his other hand flagrantly rubbing his crotch.

That was when the twenty-year-old simply blurted, "Munir said you like to do homosexual things." I refused to answer the question. I have to admit, I felt vulnerable, even if the mood was jovial and not antagonist toward the subject. Maybe it was okay to continue the discussion. Maybe I had little to fear. I really didn't know yet.

I used the Islam trick again, asking how they could be open about such things in Afghanistan. One young man chimed, "Not under the Taliban, but Afghanistan is a democracy now, we can talk about anything we want." For a second I thought that perhaps I should just ask if they wanted me here for sex. One on one, each of these former freedom fighters would indeed have been a handsome temptation, but in a group setting like this, I was unsure. What control would I have of the situation once something started? I had no idea where I even was. Visions of being gang-raped entered my mind, passed around as a party favor at an Afghan orgy. Would the women come to my aid, or was this a usual occurrence? I wondered if my curiosity, an important virtue in any travel journalist, had finally gotten the best of me.

We danced around topics until I realized I had little to fear. They were curious about many aspects of me, besides homosexuality. They were insistent I sleep there, but I still felt I needed to be vigilant about my personal safety. In a country that at the time had no banks, I had $1,000 cash on me. Munir's brother was the most persistent, letting me know how happy he would be if I lied beside him for the night. "If you stay here, you are sure to have a ball," he said. In the morning, he promised, we would get up early and do exercises with each other. He began doing martial arts moves to show off what he knew from the army. Macho and soft at the same time.

Then the men did an odd thing, completely changing the mood. They asked if I would like to watch a movie, taking out what they called a jihad video. The cover had a Chechen rebel superimposed over the Twin Towers exploding. That was jarring enough, but the violent video showed gun-toting rebels raging in a rubble-filled city and bloodied Russians rotting in the snow. A frat house mood ensued as the men watched, cheering and shouting. I wondered why they had put such a thing in, and again, I was unsure what was going on. Was this supposed to turn me on for sex? Or was it riling them up for something else?

In spite of their pleas, I knew I should go. I figured I would relieve myself first, and when I went to the outhouse, many of the men offered to escort me. Abdul took my hand, saying he would be my bodyguard, yet a small entourage of the men followed us. The outhouse was just a small, covered building in the junk-strewn, overgrown courtyard. Inside, there was a raised mud floor with a hole in the center, enormous cockroaches swarming and feeding around the edges of it. I wanted to pee and get out; I could not imagine having to spend any length of time in there. Just as I was zipping up, having taken so long from the indecision of whether to go or not, one of the men called me on the cell to ask if there was anything he could do for me, laughter in the background. As we left, we scared their backyard rooster and, fittingly, Munir asked, "that's a cock, isn't it?"

"Yes," I responded, "but the word means other things too in English." He appeared oblivious to my answer, but, still, he must have known the other meaning, or I am sure he would never have asked such a question.

It was easy to find a ride into town from one of their friends, and I piled into the backseat between Munir and Abdul. Again I wondered what I was getting into—midnight in Kabul with four men I really didn't know. As we drove in the dark, Abdul said Munir was an Al-

Qaeda member. I must make it clear that Afghan men commonly say this as a joke to test visitors, but in this situation, and with the rest of the conversation in Dari, I started to wonder. I would not say I was afraid, simply confused, though the thought that I could easily be chopped up and thrown out along these darkened roads, never to be identified, kept passing through my mind. Yet I had no choice but to trust in the situation. As the central streets of Kabul came into view outside the window, I relaxed, putting my hands on their knees to let them know I was comfortable.

As I said good-bye, hugging and kissing them in front of the Mustafa, Munir's brother still wanted me to sleep with him. I then asked Munir, "How often do you have parties in that room?"

"All the time," he said, and I told him I'd return. I still had three more nights in Kabul.

The next day, I had another interesting interaction, this time in front of a mosque. A group of construction workers was in front, taking a break. One was in traditional clothing leaning against the mosque walls, making an ideal picture, the kind you'd see in *National Geographic*. His friends joined in as I photographed him. One was particularly handsome and hammed for the camera, essentially taking over the shoot. In any other country he might have been discovered as a model, but this was Kabul, where cameras cared to focus only on terrifying looking men to titillate audiences back home.

A crowd of perhaps twenty men gathered, many of them ancient, toothless, and turbaned, and quickly realized I was gay, based on my interest in this man. Yet it was not a problem and they tried to get us together. They spoke virtually no English, but knew enough to shout "Two dollars you fuck me, you fuck me." Some of the men pushed us together, one even asking, "You like homosex?" They were so open about the possibility of a sexual exchange that it shocked me. Yet through it all, it was treated in a positive, fun manner. And in front of a mosque. I gave the young man my cell number, to the delight of the old matchmakers, but he never called.

I returned to Munir's house two days later to a smaller, more intimate gathering. In fact, it was just him, Abdul, Ali, Syed, and another friend. Things quickly went to a sexual level and it became a massage party with Ali and Abdul dueling for me. Syed might have been my intended, but he'd lost interest. Though it never happened, Munir continually dared me to kiss his brother. Each time, Abdul pulled away at the last minute, laughing. To make me look Afghan, they put a wrap on my head and we all danced. They wanted to dance with their guns too, and in spite of what interesting photos that would have made, I told them not to. In their revelry, who knows if the guns would have gone off by accident, and I worried all the more too what would happen if pictures of myself with strange Afghan men partying with guns got into the wrong hands in the West.

It got more weird and decadent as the night progressed. Munir dared me to show my penis, but when I did, everything stopped. Ali moved away from me and told me to put my pants back up, exclaiming it was a "shameful thing." When I asked what then was the purpose of being here, Munir said, "just to have fun." I was only more confused and I asked, "What do you do at these parties?"

This was when I learned the secret. Munir explained that in a group setting, he could not do anything. "If two people are together, and there is no one there, then, there are things. . . ." He kept that vague, his answer trailing off, but I said, "Here there are four witnesses?" remembering the sharia, or Islamic rule, of four witnesses to adultery. Perhaps the same applied to sex between men.

After the misunderstanding, we wandered the neighborhood, full of people and music for the Islamic weekend which began on Thursday evenings. Weddings were newly bursting on the streets and we went to visit a few ceremonies, staying on the men's sides of these open-air celebrations. Abdul and I held hands as we walked along, exchanging tender glances. Yet when we returned to the house, it was Ali I would be with.

The cushions were rearranged and everyone simply lay on one under a blanket. They all started giggling, and it was like being at a teen slumber party. Ali chose a cushion far from the others, behind a curtain and motioned for me to come over. Remembering we could do nothing with witnesses, I thought it might provide the requisite privacy.

Ali and I lay together, caressing and holding hands, staring into each other's eyes. He was a warrior, and yet he was so tender. After awhile, he asked to penetrate me, which I absolutely would not let him do, but I countered with a request to do the same to him. He never answered, and we simply continued caressing. Still, he would now and then say, "I wish you were a girl," which I found oddly disconcerting, and made me wonder if all we were doing was displacement for affections he could not express otherwise.

At one point, Ali got up and asked me to go the bathroom with him. There would have been no witnesses, but alone with such a big man, I don't think I would have had control of the situation. He pleaded with me, but I remained on the cushion and fell back to sleep. A few hours later, as dawn broke through the dust-covered window, I awoke alone. Ali had never returned. Munir said I had shamed him with rejection. I felt guilty and wished I'd taken the chance to be alone with him. So far, in spite of my apprehension, things had gone safely. Perhaps I would have had the control I was so afraid to relinquish. I will never know, and we found a car to take me back to the hotel.

I don't think I'll ever forget that night in Munir's house, but I still don't think it's enough to fully understand homosexuality in Afghanistan. The truth about many young Afghan men is that although they've lived through hardship, treat guns like fashion accessories, and murdered for their country to free it from the Taliban, strict Islamic rule means they've never seen a woman naked. They're unbelievably more naive than twelve-year-old Americans when it comes to sex. In the end, the experiences I shared with Afghan men had the feeling of 1950's teenage puppy love; we could only go so far, so many eyes around us.

Is it that they were opportunistic, being with one another if they could not have a woman, or was it that, unlike the West, they did not compartmentalize themselves, letting sexuality be what it wanted? Afghan culture is remarkably malleable, it went from progressive to conservative in a short time. From what I was seeing on this trip, the first of many to the country, it would seem the post-Taliban years had brought tremendous change, melting conservatism away on many fronts. It would be fascinating to see the country in five years, but with Western "progress," would our notions of homosexual discrimination come with it, changing Afghans as it had Afghan Americans? I wonder if I was seeing a society that simply took any form of love, including affection between men, as a wonderful thing.

My time in Kabul was perhaps the most oddly romantic time I had ever had with other men—from being wooed with flowers to stories of wartime bravery. At home, it's about money, job, house. What gay American man has a pickup line that mentions fighting against impossible odds for the freedom of his country?

The blend of homosexuality with Afghan warrior culture makes a trip here amazingly unique. Where but in Afghanistan will you be able to experience a place where men live, fight, die, and yes, even make love together as they struggle for freedom?

# Full Moon in Al Ain

*Rahal X*

In front of the mirror, I painted my eyes with kohl and rearranged my *gutra* and my *agal,* the two parts of the traditional bedouin headgear. My new off-white Omani *kandura,* the thin-clothed long robe, was almost touching the ground. Only a fine line of the colorful *usar,* a piece of cloth tied around my waist instead of underwear, was showing from underneath when I walked. It was an art form to dress bedouin style and utterly practical in this climate.

Unlike Lawrence of Arabia, I looked convincing in this outfit, and the natives considered me one of their own. This was based on two facts: my half-Arab origin, and my having been adopted by the tribe Bani Yas where I received a crash course in Islamic and classical Arabic studies to complete my truly multicultural education. The other day I had even learned how to milk a camel.

When seeing myself in the bathroom mirror in full bedu regalia, my previous life seemed very far away, as with other incarnations in different countries in Europe, Australia, and North and South America. Amina, my Egyptian mother, herself a descendant of the bedouins, would have been proud that my nomadic urges had brought me back to my Arab roots.

I wondered what my Italian father would think of his slightly eccentric son? I would never know; he died before I was born.

Suddenly the call for the Maghreb, or evening prayer, came from the minaret of the nearby mosque, interrupting my self-reflections. According to custom, I put on some perfume and joined the faithful.

The mosque was filled with numerous bedouins from the neighborhood as well as other students from the center where I was staying.

*Gay Travels in the Muslim World*
© 2007 by The Haworth Press, Inc. All rights reserved.
doi:10.1300/5481_05

Some of them were new Muslims coming from the most diverse countries, even Korea.

Since my arrival in the oasis town Al Ain near the Omani border, I too led the life of a quite orthodox Muslim. I didn't drink any alcohol. I prayed five times a day, and had thus far not indulged in any sexual activities other than masturbation, although the locals and other immigrant workers from different Arab countries, and from Iran, Afghanistan, Pakistan, and India were handsome and appealing temptations.

My new life in the United Arab Emirates was a rather striking contrast to my prior period in Barcelona. In Spain, I led the life of a Bohemian artist who was outspokenly gay, whereas here I could not wave the rainbow flag. I had to be discrete. Still, I felt totally at home with the bedouins, and these new cultural circumstances were actually rather exciting and highly inspiring. Strangely enough, here in the Arab world fitting in and being accepted was a lot easier than in most other parts of the world where I had lived. My cultural problem zones were clearly marked: it was the northern part of the globe. To be precise, the Germanic and Anglo-Saxon areas with their dry, puritan-protestant attitudes.

Not that I was a friend of the Catholic Church, but the times I spent in Spain and Latin America had been much more joyful in comparison to the ones up north. However, as far as I was concerned, nothing could beat the Islamic world. I'd been to Morocco and had also researched my Arab roots in Egypt. And ever since, after having tasted the cultural and visual sauce of my people, I got rather hooked on it. In other words, despite only being half Arab, I totally identified with this part of me. And, here on the Arabian Peninsula, I was closest to the source where Arab and Islamic culture originated.

I had no problem being a gay (at times bisexual) Muslim, and I praised Allah that I was not plagued with feelings of guilt concerning my sexuality. My argument was that Allah had created me this way in the same fashion He had created the entire universe in a spirit of diversity. He was One—and so was all of His creation, united in a state of interconnectedness—of unity within diversity. Allah is beautiful and He loves beauty. And in my eyes men were beautiful and sexually slightly more attractive than women.

My spiritual approach to life was a mystical one, one inspired by the Sufi tradition known for its tolerance and the concept of *Wahdat al-Wujud,* the unity of existence—a term coined by the followers of Muhyiddin Ibn al-Arabi, the twelfth-century Andalusian Sufi master who had brought together philosophy and mysticism and whose influence affected most authentic Sufi orders even to this day.

Another aspect that helped me develop a guilt-free sexual attitude was my Western upbringing and being a product of a time of gay liberation and human rights spreading across the planet.

When I came out of the mosque it was already dark, yet it was still very hot. I loved the heat, and here at the edge of town where the desert began the night had a special quality of peace and silence. Time was experienced in a different way. Somehow I felt caught in a sensual slow-motion movie.

I lit a cigarette and drifted into fantasies. The environment was conducive to this. But unlike other nights in which I contented myself with dreams, this time I was overcome by restlessness, and I spontaneously decided to walk to the main road leading to the center of Al Ain. After fifteen minutes, a taxi came by and I jumped in.

*"Min fadluk, fil souk,"* I said to the driver. "Please drive me to the market."

He was an older Pakistani man with a long and flaming beard dyed with henna who only nodded with his head and took off on high speed. A huge *tasbeeh,* an Islamic rosary, was hanging from the inside car mirror and an old cassette of Qawwali Sufi music almost made the speakers burst. The singer was ecstatic and the effect entrancing.

Al Ain's buildings were mostly modern with Arab-style facades, and the streets were busy with traffic and people going to restaurants and the still-open shops. It was a multicultural, but mainly Oriental, environment with very few Western people in sight.

I got out of the taxi at the souk area on the other side of town and had dinner in a Lebanese restaurant. The waiter, dressed in modern Western clothes was cute. While taking my order he discretely flirted with me in a most charming way typical to Middle Eastern men. Ron, a slightly heavy, middle-aged, American gay guy living in Al Ain passed by on the street and saw me at the table. He came inside to sit and have a coffee with me while I ate. He worked in the local hospital, and in his very American way he stood out in this environment, like a truly exotic bird, with his heavy Southern accent.

"How are you doing these days?" he inquired, the entire time checking out the men passing on the street.

"I'm fine and quite happy," I replied. "What about you?"

"Honey," he said, "I'm in hog heaven because I just had an Omani visitor with a monster meat."

Ron was a notorious and obsessed size queen. At the same time, he projected a warm and loving vibration, like an earth mother with whom one could talk about any subject. But he would always come back to his favorite theme: the dimensions of male genitals. He came across as a surreal gay cartoon character and a quite funny one at that. Ron was also a fountain of information who had been around long enough to know the local scene in great detail.

"Hail Mary," he said, almost bursting with enthusiasm, "look at that number! Big nose—big hose!"

A handsome young bedouin was crossing the street. Indeed he had a classic Semitic nose.

"Have you checked out the oasis gardens behind the souk?" Ron continued.

"Not yet," I answered.

"Well, honey, perhaps after dinner you should go there for a walk. Anything could happen in that place, and sometimes it does."

With a wicked smile Ron left. He lived right around the corner. I finished the meal, paid the cute waiter, and crossed the souk section. The call for the night prayer was blasting through town and I entered the nearest mosque. After the ritual, I threw in a petition to the Most High to soon find a friend and lover—or at least have some sensual fun for a change.

My current scenario felt a bit out of balance—it was dominated by studies and spirituality. And I recalled the Sufi saying: "We are in this world but not of it." I definitely felt the time was right to do something for my worldly existence, to speak the needs of my body. After all, Islam did not have a monkish tradition. Therefore, I decided to follow Ron's advice and check out the ancient part of the oasis.

Minutes later I was in another time zone, walking through the quiet alleys surrounded by mud walls dividing the seemingly endless oasis garden. Palm trees grew everywhere, and I could hear water running in the fountains. By now the full moon had risen up in the sky, beautifully illuminating the images before me.

It felt as if I were walking inside a 3-D Orientalist painting from the past—like an *A Thousand and One Nights* cliché. The smell of lush vegetation and humid earth filled the still-hot air while a gentle breeze moved the palm trees, causing a subtle rustling. Otherwise, all was silent, and I kept walking, getting lost in dreamtime.

But just then a hand was placed with force on my shoulder. It was no dream but very real. Before I knew it I was turned around and a tall Afghan in Pashtun tribal gear pulled me toward himself. He had a moustache and a short beard. His black eyes were fixed on mine in a hypnotic stare. He was smiling in a friendly way, showing off sensual lips and shining white teeth. The tip of his tongue quickly licked his lips before he kissed me with great passion.

There was no discussion if I was in the mood for it or not. Luckily I found this unexpected stranger rather handsome and surrendered to the kissing. He pulled up my *kandura,* then the *usar,* and rubbed his slender body against my nakedness. With one hand he caressed my face, and with the other he pulled down his pants.

His enormous hard-on pressed against mine. Very gently, but with great determination, he turned me around, and while leaning against the mud wall, he entered me. Then he grabbed my cock and we came gloriously at the same time. And then we kissed again, as passionately as we had done before.

*"Ya habibi, anta helu! Alf shukaran!"* he said in Arabic. "Oh my darling you are beautiful! A thousand thanks!"

He quickly stuffed some dirham notes in the breast pocket of my kandura and kissed me once more.

"I'm not a prostitute," I protested, deeply offended.

"It is a present," said the Afghan, "given out of gratitude."

He refused taking it back, kissed me once more, and disappeared as fast as he had appeared. I rearranged my clothes and decided to return to the souks. At the next turn of the small alley, my way was blocked. There were about fifteen Afghan tribal men, all with huge white turbans and all very handsome like my previous friend. They had the same intense stare in their lustful eyes. And each had an expression that said, "I'm next!"

The bedouins are said to be wild, but an Arab had told me that the Afghans are even wilder and much more crazy. I had to be careful; this was potentially dangerous. By no means was I in the mood to be gang-raped. I wasn't a child of sadness and certainly not an innocent from the countryside, but I had no intention of making my body turn into a public institution to please the sex-hungry crowds in this neighborhood.

My mind was running on high speed, trying to work out tactics to save my ass. Having had an actor's training in the United States, I pretended I changed my mind, and in a very cool and casual way I slowly turned around walking away in the opposite direction. After the alley's turn I began to run. It was difficult with the long bedouin robe getting in my way.

Stumbling and almost falling over, I arrived a few turns later at a dead end, my way blocked by a mud wall. Had I worn jeans I could have jumped over it and escaped through the oasis garden. I turned around to see if the Afghans were following me, but there was nobody in sight. I lit a cigarette and waited while praying to Allah to get me out of this situation.

Three cigarettes later, I decided to take the risk and return the way I had come. Perhaps the Afghans had given up and gone home? While walking, I kept praying, "Ya Fattah! Oh, Opener up of the way!" My heart was beating like crazy and I was very scared. Slowly, I turned the corner, and with great horror I saw the Afghans still standing in their original position. None of them had disappeared or even moved an inch.

They were only twenty meters away from me and I was coming closer with each step. In a sudden inspiration, Allah as the Friend provided a plan of action. I lifted up my kandura to run faster and loudly screamed, *"Allahu Akbar!* God is Great!" Then I ran as fast as I could right into the crowd of surprised Afghans who didn't expect any of this. With the help of the Most High, I managed to reach the souk section unharmed.

I stumbled upon Ron, sitting in a café, watching out for big-nosed men.

"Honey," he asked, "did you find a friend in the oasis?"

"I did," I said, "but his tribal buddies were after me as well."

"During full moon in Al Ain you got to watch out," said Ron. "They all get wired up like werewolves."

# ❧ 6                         Tenth Story Love Song
*Joe Ambrose*

## TANGIER 2001

"Tangier has been mentioned in history for three thousand years.
And it was a town, albeit a queer one, when Hercules, clad in his
loincloth, landed here four thousand years ago."

Mark Twain
*The Innocent Abroad,* 1869

I had a rough time in Marrakesh. My previous visits had to do with
music, specifically to do with filming the Gnoua Brotherhood, a semi-
covert Sufi sect who play percussion-based Moroccan trance tunes full
of throbbing sensuality. The somewhat animistic Gnoua are outsiders, vaguely distrusted by conventional Islam. That's why I like them.

It was late October 2001 and I was one month into my Moroccan
sojourn. I'd arrived on September 17th, just as every Westerner in the
country was fleeing in a state of terror born out of guilt. I'd been visiting the difficult and ornery kingdom for almost ten years, and now
planned on buying a house there. As soon as I'd rented a city-center
apartment in Tangier and decked it out to my liking, I traveled south
to Marrakesh, where I took a room for two weeks. In Marrakesh I was
kidnapped once by a gang of sex-trade criminals and, on another,
darker, occasion, was fed Rohypnol, known locally as Rosina, in the
comfort of my own room. I woke up the morning after my drugging,
lying on my bed with my trousers down around my ankles. My laptop
was gone, as was the Donna Karan jacket that my mother admired so
much every time I wore it when I sat by her deathbed four months
earlier. I don't think I was raped. I'd never been sodomized before. I

*Gay Travels in the Muslim World*
© 2007 by The Haworth Press, Inc. All rights reserved.
doi:10.1300/5481_06

think I'd have had a sense of the event if my thief cornholed me in the medina.

That afternoon, gathering my dignity around me, I got money from an ATM and packed my bags. My thief was smart enough to leave me my passport and my bank card. He knew that I'd have had to go to the cops if he'd totally thieved me—there was no way the consulate would've helped me out without a police report. He also knew that given the bedroom circumstances in which I'd been robbed I was unlikely to approach Morocco's venal, hostile police unless I really had to.

Via an eleven-hour, midnight-train journey crisscrossing Morocco's Atlantic coastal spine, I returned frantically to my Tangier home. They say Tangier feeds on the flesh of strangers. It has taken a few bites out of me. It is a city that the Moroccan National Tourist Office calls The Jewel of the North. A more accurate appellation might be The Sewer of The North. It's a sex-and-drugs city. But you have to bring your own rock 'n' roll.

I'd paid six month's rent on a decent apartment on Rue de la Liberte, a relatively chic street that houses art galleries, antique shops, and the famous El Minzah Hotel where Cecil Beaton took 1960's poolside photographs of Mick Jagger and where Genet used to swan around in his dirty pajamas. I was located within ten minutes walk of the locales who inhabit *Naked Lunch,* William Burroughs's searing howl of a novel spewed up from within the bowels of opiate and sex-infested Tangier. From my window I could see Dean's Bar, the dodgy gay hangout where all those long-ago American bohos hung out and organized their exploitation of the local youths. Nowadays, it's a squalid home to Tangier's indigenous sex hounds and to some dangerously rough trade. I never visited Dean's Bar, but I had heard the reports.

I had a contract from a publisher to write a hardback biography of punk icon Iggy Pop. I was one third of the way through that task, but in the light of what happened in Marrakesh I was seriously thinking about finishing the job back in London, my safe European home. I was in no humor for company or for liaisons of any kind. While I decided my next move, I put my head down and got on with writing about Iggy.

Two days later I was breakfasting late at the Cafe de Paris, reading a Maigret novel, when I first met Krim. I kind of glanced him out of the corner of my eye passing by my Boulevard table. God knows what brought him to my attention but, knowing him like I do now, he'd probably been casing me and sizing me up since I'd arrived at the café. For all I know, he may have been sizing me up for the previous five years. No doubt he'd been prancing up and down in front of the café for at least half an hour, waiting for me to wake up and put aside my paperback. He was a patient worker. Being a retired, top-of-the-range, Tangier rent boy, his intelligent researching and his bovine strolling up and down Tangier's trade-infested boulevard was the main part of his work. He'd gotten to work on me. I liked him then, and, despite everything, I like him still. More important than my conditional affection is the mild fascination that he still exerts over me.

When he caught me looking at him he didn't flinch, but adopted a sort of ridiculous, corny, James Dean–style stance under a nearby lamppost, one knee cocked and his head resting against the metal pole. A lonely old guy might've been impressed if that old guy wasn't used to much by way of sex glamour. I wasn't old or lonely, so I wasn't interested, just irritated that he was now staring back at me. He was short, which doesn't do anything for me, and he looked like shit, pale skinned and puffy in tired, worn-out, head-to-toe, bootleg Nike. The very essence of urban inelegance. I didn't make him right away for a junkie but I had him down as shabby, poor, unglamorous, not my style.

He moved in my direction to stand in front of my table, politely asking in nonaccented English if he could sit with me for a moment. I'm always willing to hang out with hustlers, having my own petty background in petty crime. I've always enjoyed their zany nihilism or bad attitudes. I said he could sit down, but that I was leaving in fifteen minutes. He proceeded to bore me for the next half hour with a variety of routines, obviously tried and tested a thousand times on a thousand men, intended to extract terribly modest amounts of money from lonesome foreigners who sat alone outside the Cafe de Paris looking at lean teenagers in shell suits.

Ten dirhams is roughly a dollar. He needed fifty dirhams to pay his monthly gym fees, his proposition confirmed by a quick flash of impressively muscular calves. "Good, huh?" he enquired gutturally, slapping his left thigh as he looked around to make sure that nobody noticed this exposition. No doubt the sight of a little taut flesh normally did the trick. For three hundred dirhams he knew a man who'd hide him in the back of a truck and smuggle him into Spain. For fifty dirhams he could get me some very good heroin. For one hundred dirhams a week he would be my housekeeper or secretary. He'd help me find a good apartment, the meaning of life, the café where Mick Jagger once smoked a joint, maybe even the secret of eternal youth. I told him to go back to the Jagger café and await the singer's return. I advised him that Jagger would pay him good money for this secret of eternal youth and might even subsidize his gym fees.

Krim actually knew who Jagger was—not necessarily the case with all the Tangier street hustlers who'll promise to whisk you off to Stones-related sites—so he was familiar with Mick's Peter Pan disposition and got my joke. But he was way too desperate for money and too in need of a fix to be truly amused by my offhand dismissal of his desperate scams. We were going nowhere together. I didn't want him around me on any level and he was pitching me tired tawdry concepts. You don't have a duty to support all the junkies in the world just because you defend their right to be junkies.

I determined that maybe I'd give him something if I could succinctly debrief him, Paul Theroux, big-shot-travel-writer style, about the facts and figures of his life. I write, so I'm a voyeur. I like to look.

How long had he been working as a whore? Since he was sixteen, and now he was twenty-five. He wanted to know if I'd ever heard of a certain, now dead, publishing magnate, famous for his friendship with an actress known for her weight problem. I nodded knowingly that everybody'd heard of him. Krim explained to me that when he was only seventeen the man used to give him fifty dollars every time the he visited his palace. What did Krim have to do for the money? The distinguished man liked to suck Krim's cock.

What did his mother think he did for a living? She thought he worked as a guide with tourists. If his clients permanently resided in

Tangier, and he lived in, he told her that he worked as a gardener or general houseboy. He also did undertake such jobs. By the time I got to know him he was making adult efforts to quit hustling. He was very good at getting drugs—any drug—on demand for foreigners. He knew how to install bootleg satellite television dishes so they could watch five hundred television channels when not taking drugs, having sex, or gossiping about one another. Sometimes, of course, they did all four things at the same time. Krim also knew how to rent apartments, talk good bullshit, get you a pay-as-you-go mobile phone, and imperceptibly extract your money from your pocket. He was useful.

I wanted to know how he could handle all the loveless and lustless sex. He said that he was used to it now. He'd been a very shy boy, recently arrived in town from Asilah, a small fishing resort half an hour's drive south of Tangier. The first time a man pulled down his trousers—when he was fifteen—he felt very bad about it. He'd been working at the Fes Market food souk, one of the sensual wonders of the Islamic world, since he was thirteen. There, amid the dappled light, the scared caged monkeys, the snakes and lizards both real and metaphorical, he got to know the likes of Paul Bowles, Tangier's preeminent prose stylist and sexual predator. He used to see my old pal Hamri, Morocco's national painter and the man who originally invited me to Tangier, fussily purchasing oranges and bananas. He said Hello, *Bonjour,* and *Salaam Alaikum* to a cross section of upmarket Tangerine society. He was a bag carrier, hauling stuff back to people's cars or to their homes, living well off tips.

One day he carried bags to a large, flashy Mercedes owned by a somewhat Asian-looking Frenchman who turned out to be a big shot in Tangier's royal palace—an assistant chamberlain or whatever. This guy told Krim that a job was available in the palace gardens if he wanted to improve himself. The following afternoon he made his way to the palace where his benefactor initiated him into life at court and life on the mattress. He stayed there a year working in the gardens, leading a gilded fantasy life unimaginable to the average working class Moroccan youth. During that time he met the crown prince, the current Moroccan king. He developed a taste for high life accessed through his good looks and steady intelligence. He got kicked out when his boss traded him in for a new model, also sourced from among the pretty Fes Market urchins. By then he knew how to behave in front of the rich and he knew how to make easy money selling his young ass while trying to hold on to his old soul.

A long phase of Krim as upmarket party boy commenced. He made big money—a lot more money than I was making at the same time in London—and he spent that money on drugs. Heroin was no problem so long as he was earning more in a month than his truck-driving father earned in a year. By the time he approached me at the Cafe de Paris the glory days were long gone. The rent boy scene in Tangier is rabidly competitive and youth is at a premium. You can get anything you want—boy or girl—from the age of five up for a very modest amount of money. A guy in his midtwenties with a junk interface is well past his sell-by date. That's why we were having our rather desperate and tedious October 2001 conversation.

He was loitering around the Cafe de Paris because an old Moroccan man whom he didn't much like had arranged to meet him there with a view to going to a nearby hotel room for a session. The old guy was going to give him a hundred dirhams for a blow job. He was dreading the transaction.

"When he is finished he likes to take me to a bar for a drink so he can look into my eyes, knowing I've had his filthy cock in my mouth. That's the best part for him, the part when I feel worse than a dog and he knows he is the boss." Until he'd fallen on hard times he'd never gone with Moroccans, always foreigners. They paid better and, in any case, if he avoided doing business with locals, word wouldn't get around the big village of Tangier that he was a rent boy.

So he thought. When I got to know him I saw that he imagined himself terribly adept, subtle, and ahead of the game. The teenage Krim was all of those things, but the man I got to know was punch-drunk, punked out, on the ropes, and a servant to his addiction.

I was mellowing toward him—he could tell a story and I've always been a sucker for a guy who can spin a yarn. Then I snapped out of it, reminding myself of the morning, three days earlier when I woke in a stupor, sticking my finger up my asshole to make sure that there were no cuts or abrasions. With that pungent memory rising up to greet me I gave him fifty dirhams, which he clearly felt was mighty slim pickings, and headed for my apartment.

Three days later he saw me at the café again. I was unimpressed when he reprised his gym fees story, but, once more, I was cajoled into some level of interest. I was getting over Marrakesh. He looked much better; he'd had a fresh haircut. He said he was a good cook and offered to come make a tagine for me in my apartment. I agreed to this for the following evening, gave him some money for himself and for the tagine ingredients. The last thing I said before he left was, "But remember, Krim, we'll have food. And talking. No money. No sex. You understand? No sex."

In the half hour after he left me three separate men—all of them known to me as the most disreputable vipers in Tangier—approached me and told me to have nothing to do with him.

"That one he go with old men," advised one.

"He steal everything you have, my friend, he send you home naked to your own people," confided another.

"He sick boy. He very sick boy," opined a third, theatrically furrowing his brows with an implication of ominous foreboding. Now I was curious.

We took it from there. Dinner went well, we talked for six hours, and he left without a struggle, no more than a taxi fare in his pocket. The next day we talked for another four or five hours, and I let him crash on a couch in the salon. The third day I cooked the dinner. He moved in permanently within a week. He kept to the couch while I kept to the bedroom. There was also the matter of heroin.

"Ten Story Love Song" by The Stone Roses was the pivotal drug soundtrack to that time in my life. The background noise was also Snoop Dogg, Gregory Isaacs, the Ghost Dog soundtrack, Dylan bootlegs, Johnny Cash, Missy Elliot, the Stones, and Slipknot. I made it my business to listen to none of the Sufi music that had attracted me to Morocco in the first place. I wasn't tired of that pulsating throb—indeed I continued to collect Sufi cassettes—but, via Krim, I immersed myself in an Arabic-speaking Islamic society. Four months passed during which time I never met a native English speaker or a Christian. Retreating into the music of my own tribe, the punk/hip-hop stuff of my European urban life, was an anchor. (I also disappeared most afternoons into the life of Iggy Pop, writing quickly about a long-expired New York world of junkies, transvestites, and radical deviants from the norm.)

Krim gave me two gifts. Three weeks into our cohabitation he presented me with an impressive English translation of the Koran published in paperback by Penguin. He'd been given this by one of his more benign clients back in the halcyon days. The mind boggled; some guy got a hand job from a teenager and gave the kid the holiest text of his religion as a thank-you.

Just before I returned to London Krim gave me a set of what he called Islamic jewelry. Dubious, I quizzed him a lot as to exactly what he meant by "Islamic jewelry," because the gold-plated cuff links, tie pin, and medallion on a chain that I got in a black velveteen case seemed to be pretty much your average flashy Arab tack. Eventually he brought an Osama photograph, popular on T-shirts and posters across Morocco, to my attention. His hero was indeed decked out in a set of trinkets similar to the gear he'd given him. No doubt Osama's stuff was made out of real gold

Late at night when the city was closing down, I read that Koran a great deal, watching the harbor lights from my window, listening to gangs of hooligan boys roaming dark, deserted streets four floors down, Rai tunes blaring out of all-night sandwich joints. My favorite Koran quote was, "As for the unbelievers, Allah can surely do without them." I took to quoting this at the various charlatans and reprobates who hung around the Cafe de Paris hunting for tourist victims. "Ah, yes." they'd murmur gently, not entirely sure what I was on about.

We sometimes talked religion in the late afternoon when I took a break from Iggy and before he descended into junk rapture. He reckoned that two topics never mentioned in the Koran, a work he claimed to be intimate with, were heroin and homosexual sex. He was confident that Allah had no opinion, good bad or indifferent, on these matters. He talked of a malevolent Islamic djinn or evil spirit who comes in the night to your bed and holds you tight so that you can't breathe or move. I wanted to be visited by this djinn, but he never manifested. Another time Krim wanted to know, "What is the attraction of the forbidden?" I told him, "the attraction of the forbidden is that it is forbidden."

He kept a little black book which was literally a little black notebook in which he'd carefully written down all the details he had on each and every client he'd known. Phone numbers, home addresses, jobs, other connections. One of these was an English knight who'd been given his knighthood by the Queen for his work in the area of child protection. He'd made a special study of vulnerable kids in care homes and orphanages. When in Tangier this Knight of the Realm, a veritable Robin Hood to abuse victims everywhere, lived with an eleven-year-old boy in a large villa in which he organized orgies for other members of the British establishment who visited town.

Then it was time for Ramadan. Things get desperate and very cold in Tangier during the holy month. Money ceases to circulate, so the poor have it tough. Many homeless die or go into decline. One bitter night I had to go meet Krim's penniless brother Karim outside an art deco cinema on the Grand Socco because he had a nice pair of Nike that he wanted to sell me. I liked Karim, a good-looking, dashing thug in his late twenties, trying to go straight after life as a big-time armed robber. The trainers, which were cool, not bootlegs, new, obviously thieved, a good price, didn't fit. I gave him some money and he slouched off into the night like a languid panther.

Krim learned how to use my new laptop and wrote a long and interesting essay that began, "I have heard many other stories which I enjoyed very much and I have also told a lot of stories which he really enjoyed them. We laugh about our stories because some of them were funny and then we became closer and good friends."

I took the two hour ferry to Gibraltar, a very strange time warp of an English town just across the Strait of Gibraltar, because my London mail had been forwarded to a Gib convenience address. I changed from my now-threadbare Moroccan street gear into plane traveling clothes, regular-guy casuals I use to smuggle my drugs around the world. Krim, when he saw me decked out like a white man, was convinced that I was skipping town and nothing I could say would reassure him.

After two uneventful days in Gib—the highlight being a shoe shop sale at which I picked up loads of Converse All Star trainers for next to nothing—I took a nighttime ferry back to Tangier. We all nearly died on that journey, our small hovercraft mercilessly buffeted by thirty-foot waves of violent black water. By the time we reached safe harbor I'd been in a state of morbid fear for so long that every stitch I was wearing was sweat soaked. My legs were so weak from terror that I could scarcely carry myself to a taxi, never mind up the four flights of stairs that awaited me on Rue de la Liberté.

I could smell the beer and sense the party when I opened the door to hear a conversation going on in French while dippy jazz-funk-soul music came out of the speakers. I sauntered into the salon to find a very drunk Krim entertaining this seedy, middle-aged French guy in a cheap suit who'd obviously paid for all the now-empty Heineken and Coors cans that lay in small piles on the floor, surrounded by crumpled-up Marlboro packets and bits of joints in puddles of sour beer. As I made my way into the bedroom to dump my bag I glared at the French guy—the sort of glare that looks like its going to be followed up three seconds later by a solid right hook.

Krim came into the bedroom, laughing, to tell me that it wasn't what it seemed to be. I tore a new asshole out of him right there, explaining that he should never ever bring his tricks back to my place.

"Aah, you sneak back here in the night from Gibraltar like a snake and catch me," he rasped. "But this man Claude is just a friend of mine. Nothing dirty."

Back in the salon a petrified Claude was gathering his bits and pieces about him, muttering *excusez-moi* in a tone supposed to imply that we were both sophisticated white men caught up in some baroque Third World scenario not entirely of our own making. I don't know why I was so annoyed. He just looked like a real meat-beater. If he wanted to entertain Tangier's top rent boy, retired, he should've rented an apartment to go with the boy.

Twenty minutes after Claude's departure Krim sulked off into the night. Some Moroccans enjoy a good fight, but he didn't. I subsequently found out what Claude was really up to. He was in the process of legally adopting Krim's nine-year-old cousin, a boy whose mother,

Krim's aunt, was a professional heroin smuggler. Claude was offering $5,000 for the kid. Krim said that he was opposed to the deal—which never came off. I think.

With Krim temporarily out of the way, I slipped into a white djellaba and headed for an opening at Galerie Delacroix, the French Consulate–connected gallery around the corner from my place. There I met a farouche teenager called Said, well dressed in a brown djellaba, a rich kid with a good Swatch and real D&G trainers. He reckoned that we were attending *"un exposition inutile."* I agreed, so we headed back to the apartment, where he spent the night listening to Snoop Dogg, smoking hash, and asking me questions such as, "It say in the Bible that there are three Gods, yes?" He had a giggling poise that a member of the underclass like Krim could only dream about.

At the end of February I decided that I wanted to go back to my own culture. They didn't need me in Morocco, I knew I wasn't going to buy a house there, and the Iggy book was almost done. Krim said that I was right to go home but I could tell that he thought, correctly, that I was deserting him. My role was to give him shelter from the storm during a bleak winter when there were no other foreigners around. When I was leaving he said, "I am from the Boulevard and you're from Hollywood. Please don't forget me."

Later his brother Karim was murdered around the corner from the family home. He was stabbed six times and probably died quickly. Krim discovered his body the following morning, lying on his back, his proud arms raised to the sky, his mouth wide open, his eyes open.

Eventually, Krim did nine months for some fancy swindle that went wrong. I visited Tangier while he was locked up and discovered that he'd ripped me off for about $5,000, while we were living together, in circumstances that are a whole other story. I was impressed by the aplomb with which he managed his seamless transgression. I take my hat off to him; I'm enough of a cheat and a fraudster to grimace wryly and put it down to experience. Last week he sent me an e-mail that said, "Don't trust anybody with your money. Not even me."

I see him every time I go to Morocco. He survives. I just don't know what will happen to him. I won't ever forget him.

## *BOY BOY*

Frank and I called him Boy Boy because he was wearing a "Boy" T-shirt the first time we met him on Place Djemma El Fna in Marrakesh. That was just ten years ago though everything has changed beyond recognition since then. He looked about twelve but was, I think, fourteen. He wanted dirhams from us to play video games in the arcade located in the basement of the café in which we hung out, adjacent to one of the important El Fna mosques. He'd been given the T-shirt by a European man. When we explained to him that "boy" was the English for *garcon* he said, in his breaking adolescent voice, *"Je ne suis pas un garcon. Je suis un homme."* He made a big impression on the two of us, a nice, smart kid with a loveable face and some street smarts. His best friend was a glue sniffer, also nice, but neither smart nor pretty.

Those early visits to Marrakesh were largely to do with the Gnoua Brotherhood with whom we were working. In more recent years I've gone back alone, once renting a medina apartment that I didn't much like, principally staying at the CTM Hotel which is right on El Fna. I always get to see Boy Boy at some stage during my visit—he's street life and I've been addicted to street life since I was eight.

When he was sixteen he was a full-time, ace-face rent boy, obviously in the grip of some drug addiction because all he frantically wanted to talk about was doing business. He never quite took it on board that I was only interested in him from a friendship point of view. There was no talking to him then. When I said I wanted to take some photographs he thought I meant dirty photographs, seemed pleased that I'd finally seen sense. I explained that I just wanted to take some pictures of him walking around El Fna. Then he obviously thought I was weird, but he showed up the next day on time with a fresh haircut and his best shirt on. That was the only time during my visit that he seemed to be the same nice kid who me and Frank hung out with just a few years earlier. He was somber and petulant as he posed, taking the photographs very seriously. He told me that something very unpleasant had happened to him the night before but he wouldn't say what. He didn't look too great at that time in his life—he looked worn out. I wondered if I'd ever see him alive again.

Eighteen months later he'd come through that rather frantic stage though he was still on the game. He told me that his real name was Taha, that Mustafa was just his rent boy nom de guerre. He looked much better, healthy, with the makings of a big ass, and looked a little like a member of one of those Paisley Underground bands, complete with check-patterned bell bottoms and paisley shirt. He was fun to hang around with again even though he was drinking heavily. When I showed him the photographs I'd taken during our prior encounter he had no recollection of meeting me or of doing the photographs. We went to the movies often—he liked martial arts films and shouted his encouragement during the fight scenes. He told me that he'd tried girls and didn't like them, that he preferred men. This time around the only problem was that he was surrounded by heavy, pimp-style individuals obviously trying to take advantage of his film-star good looks and exuberant personality. They assumed that I was one of his tricks and that the two of us were doing business without including them in on the deal. There was an ironic feeding frenzy—when poor people think they're being done out of money they lose it.

I saw Taha two days ago. He's now a tough-looking young man, hanging around close to Hotel de Paris, one of the more expensive hotels near El Fna. He works with a gang of tourist hustlers waiting for the busloads of suckers who now decamp in front of Hotel de Paris—they used to stop on El Fna but traffic is now barred from there. He has followed a typical trajectory for young Moroccan petty criminals. The starring roles end when you're twenty, you get good supporting roles later. It's irrevocably downhill all the way by the time you're thirty.

I don't think happiness comes into it, but, no doubt, he was happy playing those forgotten video games. He was already a man back then.

# My Intifada
*Ethan Pullman*

1998 was the year I began my intifada. Until then, I was a Palestinian and a Muslim. That year, I came out, adding Homosexual to my identity. I knew that I would, at best, be severing any future interaction or communication with family. I still know that there's a constant threat of honor killing by a family member, or falling victim to some archaic Middle East sodomy law, should I travel to that region wearing my identity on my sleeve. Granted, the term *intifada* came to symbolize the Palestinian uprising against the Israeli occupation, but I prefer to conjure up its literal and peaceful meaning: to wake up from sleep or unconcerned status. Therefore, my intifada musters up my courage to awaken the unconcerned. But alas, a voice unheard cannot illicit change, and so I tell my story.

I was born in 1966 to Palestinian parents, on the west coast of Saudi Arabia, and raised in Riyadh until my midteens. My parents maintained family ties in the Gaza Strip, Amman, and El Qa'hira, through annual visits. In Riyadh, I received religious and secular education. I remember growing up in a relatively moderate environment. Our social circles included Syrians, Egyptians, Lebanese, Jordanians, Saudis, and the occasional foreign born and/or raised. As a result, our traditions had to be more fluid, in comparison with the more homogeneous majority, to accommodate this diversity. Nevertheless, my father as head of our household reserved the right to change the rules as he deemed fit. This often depended on perceptions of which people "mattered." I never figured out who exactly these people were.

Beginning at five and throughout puberty I picked up on many more rules that I could never quite understand or follow. Boys and girls were much more closely supervised and were rarely allowed to

*Gay Travels in the Muslim World*
© 2007 by The Haworth Press, Inc. All rights reserved.
doi:10.1300/5481_07

play together, so naturally, and fortunately for me, my playmates were males. Haanee was my closest playmate and my willing accomplice. We would play doctor, and our bond was evident but incomprehensible to either of us at that age. We were drawn to each other emotionally. The bond was strong enough that we became creative at finding opportunities to explore each other, until the day my mother walked in on us. She locked me up in the bathroom and I was subjected to a lecture and to threats of telling my father. She never followed through with her threats. Of course, my mother could have told him, but she never had the heart to do it. She figured that I had given my father enough reason to paint my olive skin black and blue. I never seemed to satisfy my father or live up to his expectations. I was always too weak, too clumsy, too irresponsible, too this, too that. Living with my father was like living at the bottom of a dormant volcano. We never figured out when we should run for cover; he had no warning signs of a pending eruption. As the eldest, I was held at the highest elevations of his volcano and, naturally, I was always the first to get caught in his outpour.

Of course there were frequent thoughts of escape, but religion and society's rules didn't allow for that. Family and group structures are intricate and central to Islam, especially where family laws are concerned. The family unit extends beyond fathers and mothers to include distant relatives. As a group, this identity is so strong that you would be hard pressed to find shelters for the displaced, such as homeless, women divorcees, orphans, and runaways, and much less for homosexuals like me. In any such case, individuals would be returned to a family member to be dealt with. Tradition expects it, and Islam supports it. I remember the day that my mother left for her brother's. She was crying because my brother, two years younger, hit her. I expected my father to fly into one of his rages and discipline my brother. Instead, my brother received nothing more than a verbal warning. To add insult to injury, instead of my brother, I was sent to fetch my mother. Fortunately, I didn't have to bear the burden of turning my mother against her will. My maternal uncle did a fine job; "Go back and pray to Allah the One," he urged her. The same Allah that said, "Honor thy mothers."

In high school, I fantasized about having a relationship, a same-sex relationship that would be at least protected, if not accepted. I developed emotional connections and even elicited sexual desires, but sexual experimentation was rare, and its discovery would have been too costly. I found myself struggling with role-playing: dominant versus passive. I hated the stigma attached with the latter, and didn't perceive myself playing either role exclusively. My mates weren't comfortable with this because it would imply that they might have to play the passive role, only *then* casting them as queer. As a result, my sexual experience during high school was very limited. I never managed to unite my sexual and emotional desires, except in my fantasies.

Then one black day a friend of my father's met me after school, claiming that my father wouldn't be picking me up that day. I was to go with him to my father's office. Pre–cell phone days, and not having a reason to suspect anything, I obliged. He decided he needed to make a stop at his office to pick up a package (supposedly going to my father) and said that I should go with him. As soon as I stepped into his office I felt an edge of cold steel pressing at my throat as he guided me with his body, from behind, to a corner. He grabbed my school bag, tossed it aside, and asked me to undress. With his knife still at my throat, I could only beg quietly. There was no one to hear my prayers (the one that did wouldn't materialize to save his servant). I remember pissing uncontrollably out of fear and desperation. How humiliating? It angered my rapist, but didn't stop him.

After an hour that seemed like an eternity, I was dropped off back at school, where my father would find me. Peeved, he asked me where I'd been. I thought of my mother. I thought of my aunt. I thought of my religious teaching. I had not a witness, much less the four required by sharia, or Islamic law, when making an accusation. So, instead, I quietly said that I went across the street to talk to a friend and that I didn't see him looking for me. I don't know if he believed me, but he never pressed. I wondered if he preferred not to know; maybe he thought it was better that way. At least my life would be spared.

My break came in 1980, when my father offered me the chance to go the United States for a summer to study English. Granted, this offer wasn't completely selfless on his part. He had a high interest in increasing my GPA (after all, the neighbor's kid managed to score a slightly higher GPA that year). Let me be clear here, I was no failure: in sixth grade I graduated first in the kingdom; by ninth grade the competition was tougher and I managed only to tie for first place, which I was reminded was not something to be proud of. In 1980 my grades predicted a GPA in the 94th percentile. A disaster! My aunt to the rescue! She happened to have the right connections that would eventually allow me to spend a summer in the United States. I jumped at the chance for temporary freedom.

Barely fifteen then, my father had to transfer "legal custody" to my host family—this was symbolic only because it gave them power of attorney should something go wrong, but had no legal implication as to their role as "adoptive parents." So any dreams of being adopted into another family had to be put on hold. Admittedly, I did not grasp the gravity of this development and how it would change my future for years to come. For the moment, though, I would be immersed in a new culture, a new set of rules, and a new way of seeing.

My summer was spent in a small city in western Pennsylvania. My attempt to fit in was met with many challenges. Most memorable was my first day of phys ed. I was asked to change into gym clothes. No problem, or so I thought. My first step into the locker room was about to entice a heart attack. I walk in and there are my classmates. Buck naked! The lockers were open space, no privacy what so ever. I was not about to risk a hard-on in front of a group of students to whose possible teasing I couldn't even attempt to respond. What was I to do? I found the divider that faces the entrance door of the locker room and planted myself between that door and the divider. There was no one there. I could quickly change and no one would know the difference. I was proud to come up with such a perfect solution. I began to undress quickly—off with shoes, socks, pants, shirt, and underwear. That was the precise moment that our gym instructor pushed the door open, displaying my nakedness to a hallway full of students. It was a while before I would live that day down. Regardless, I managed to convince my father to send me to college in the United States. My plot to escape went unnoticed, but I knew I would experience new freedoms.

In the United States, I could explore, but it was quite a revelation to realize that when it came to male bonding, the Middle East attitude was much more relaxed. Here, in the land of the free, male bonding was tricky. A gaze or touch that lingered too long and you could invite ridicule, threats, and abuse. Suddenly, I was nostalgic for the days when I walked hand in hand with my schoolmates. True, being incognito was much easier back home. However, it also gave us the luxury of introspection without having to deal with the fear of gay bashing, or deal with such imbecile activities as bullies mopping the floor with my jacket, or name-calling, or writing vulgarities on one another's desks. So much for progress! In the United States, same-sex bonding is much more strictly proscribed than back home.

Still, I was fully aware that bonding or not I had the freedom to run away, be an individual, and set my own rules. In the United States I had options: a number of shelters and programs existed to protect the victims and "misfits" like me. Others might have seen such alternatives as a sign of an ill society; I saw them as a sign of hope. Individuals could find support, strength, and healing. Death or jail no longer needed be inevitable.

College was a true education, although not the best academic experience. Personally, it combined the best and worst years of my life. There I met my would-be first love interest. There I discovered other queers. In this great institution of education, I could intellectualize what I was experiencing—you couldn't even come close to this in most of the Muslim Middle East. This was an education I was not about to pass up! I developed a network of support. Don't get me wrong, I had no clue what I wanted. I just knew I wasn't going to find this opportunity back home, and that thought sent my heart rate pulsing. I was exalted, but panic-stricken. My useless fits of hysterics and tears, too frequent to hide from my friends, were also becoming difficult to explain to my family, especially my younger brother, who was also my roommate for a period of time.

When my brother came to stay with me in the United States and to attend college we were very close. The first few years we did almost everything together. Sure our personalities were like opposite ends of the magnet, but we were one. Then he changed. Without notice, he turned conservative and became critical of every aspect of my life. He felt he had religious superiority and, therefore, a license to dictate my conduct. Before long, he would have an opinion on my choice of friends. For the most part, I ignored his nagging, until I met Michael.

Michael and I met during my first year of college and began to spend a considerable amount of time together. My brother didn't really suspect anything. Michael was out to his family and I flirted with the thought of doing the same. He knew the reason for my hesitation and never pushed the issue, so you can imagine his shock when during a telephone conversation one April I suggested that I would tell my brother. He dared me to, not to entice me, but out of disbelief.

So I turned, still on the phone, to my brother and blurted "This is Michael on the phone. He's my boyfriend; I am gay."

"Like Hell you are!" Pausing from slicing an onion, my brother pointed the knife at me.

"Well, I am. You can't change that," I said.

"Yeah, I could kill you, that's what I can do," he retorted.

"Michael, I must go. I'll call you later," I said. Michael was dumbfounded.

"You'd better," Michael replied. "You've got one hour. I need to know if you'll be alright."

I hung up the phone and looked at my brother with disbelief.

"You think you could just kill me and get away with it? Did you think about your future? You'll go to jail for the rest of your life," I told him.

"No I won't. I'd kill you and leave for Saudi Arabia. They won't persecute me there. I am defending family honor," he shot back. Realizing he was probably right, I contemplated the situation for a moment. Suddenly it occurred to me it was the first of April.

"Happy April Fool's Day," I broke out with a nervous laugh. My brother, not amused, reluctantly drew back.

"Not funny! Don't pull a stunt like that again." I never discussed this again. I never talked to Michael again either.

Years of hiding and deceit rolled by. One short affair after another, I continued plotting for escape, but there was no light at the end of my tunnel. As the end of college drew near, I realized I was running out of time. I needed to do something quickly, but what? I managed to convince my father that graduate school was necessary. To my relief, he granted me my wish. My doom was to be temporarily delayed, for another two years at least. As fate would have it, the Gulf War was being planned. The year 1991 was a turning point. As a Palestinian, I would be denied return to Saudi Arabia and Israel. I applied for asylum and was approved. I could stay. I was fortunate to have education and a good record.

But my ties with family and land were still strong. It was tolerable as long as I was single, but when I met Philip, the prospect of a happy and peaceful future lead me to consider some serious changes. In the land of the free, I was still shackled by my past. My relationship with Philip began to resemble that of Simon and Wai-Tung in *The Wedding Banquet.* Every time my father would call from the airport, I would be sent into a frenzy of hotel searches and phone calls warning Philip to "de-gay" our apartment, just in case my father insisted on paying me a visit. Oh, yes, and third roommate Janet would be recruited for "operation de-gay."

Well, you can imagine how ludicrous this became. During those times, Philip would have to cease existing in my life until my father left. Philip, bless him, never complained. I loved him for his incredible patience. Perhaps that's what kept us together for the next five years. In any case, I resigned that I could no longer put him through this. I was certain that I would lose my biological family, and possibly my "adoptive family" as well, but the alternative was killing me slowly. I resolved to come out to both.

The next call from my father, I took a deep breath and told him, in English, "I am gay." I didn't want to use an Arabic term because I couldn't conjure up a term that would contain a positive, or at least neutral, meaning. My father, still not understanding, had me explain what that meant: that I preferred the company of men. Instantly, there was dead silence, followed by my stepmother's voice. She pleaded with me to return from the "land of sin." I tried explaining that this wasn't a recent experience. I tried to explain to her what I felt as a child, as a teen, to no avail. She even suggested that my family would come and get me, take me to "sheiks" who could "exercise Satan" out of me. I told her that I would disappear where they could never find me. I was not about to become my aunt.

But when God closes one door, he opens another. Response from the adoptive family who took care of me when I was in high school was overwhelmingly touching. For one, it was Dad who reached out with assurance that I would always belong. Their love healed my wounds.

Not so long after, I changed my identity and disappeared. I re-solved to never look back or, perhaps look, but only to remember why I must go forward.

My story might not be unique by any stretch of the imagination. In fact, there's really no way to know for sure, because many homo-sexuals in the Middle East choose to remain silent, out of fear of perse-cution by governments or family, out of self-imposed loyalty, or, worst of all, out of self-hatred. But even the fortunate few who manage to escape are rarely willing to risk visibility.

As long as honor crimes, sodomy laws, and insane fatwas exist in the Muslim Middle East, there will be lives at risk. Although it is true that times are changing and greater queer visibility exists in much of that region, such visibility often fires back. To be visible in the Mus-lim Middle East is to invite persecution. That region has never been stable in the application of its laws, especially with the laws regarding sodomy. Even recent scholars who look critically at evidence to ex-plain current sodomy laws from either two of the major Islamic sources are hard pressed to reach agreement. The Holy Qur'an, the un-changed word of God, is vague at best. The hadith, which refers to a number of historical books that contain reports of sayings, actions, and examples of how the Holy Prophet Muhammad put the teachings of the Holy Qur'an into practice, is inconsistent and largely depend-ant on whose chain of transition is considered the "truer" vehicle relat-ing the tradition (Sahih Muslim and Sahih Bukhari are considered to be the truest, others such as Abu Dawood, and Ibn Hanbal are con-sidered less reliable). To be completely frank, I know that I would not have mustered the courage to leave my family were I to have re-mained living in the Middle East. In fact, I know that I frequently considered suicide as an escape, and would have actually found such action more merciful to all involved. My family would not have to deal with shame; my jury would be released from having to stand in my judgment.

To a larger extent, neither the non-Muslim nor the secular Middle East has a great record of protection from persecution. In Israel, gay Palestinians are not given asylum, leaving them at the mercy of their families. Jordan, progressive in so many ways, has not taken positive measures either. Most recently, Egypt faced international criticism for arresting fifty-two homosexuals. Saudi Arabia arrested and flogged many more. If anything, the Muslim Middle East has been aggressive in seeking out queers.

I still hear from, and speak to, many who are much more courageous than I am. I wasn't courageous enough to stay and fight; they were. Still there are many who secretly question their worth and fear for their lives. There are many who must stay silent, planning their own *intifada*. God be with you!

# Lance Corporal Key's
# Middle East Vacation

*Jeff Key*

When I was first approached to write an article for a book on gay travel in the Middle East, I thought it was a joke. "You don't understand," I said, "I went there as part of the war. It was no vacation!" In truth, compared to what some of our brave service members have witnessed over there, since I never saw combat and I was only there for a little over two months (I was flown home for surgery after a non-combat-related injury), my stay in Iraq *was* a vacation. As things get worse there every day, the effects are going to be long reaching for our men and women in uniform, not to mention for the Iraqis. Baghdad will never be the preferred "getaway" in the Middle East, not in our lifetime anyway. In fact, for most of the people in Iraq now, I would imagine that's what they would all like to do now—get away.

Then I found out the reason I was approached to write this article was because of an excerpt from my Iraq war journals in which I describe an interaction with a gay Iraqi man I met there. The following is that entry.

## THE GAY IRAQI

I stand atop my vehicle in Badrah with my weapon at the read, balancing friendly with guarded. We want the people to know we are here to help, but looking passive is an invitation to trouble. A man in his early twenties passes on the opposite side of the street. He is fit and good-looking, in that brooding, Middle-Eastern sort of way. I follow him with my eyes. As I'm watching this Iraqi soccer player walk down the street, he looks back . . . in that way. We smile at my catching him, and in a couple of minutes he's made his way over. Cpl. Manana has come back and agrees to stand "guardian angel," that's the post I'd

*Gay Travels in the Muslim World*
© 2007 by The Haworth Press, Inc. All rights reserved.
doi:10.1300/5481_08

been manning, in which one stands up high to keep a lookout over the whole crowd to make sure nothing happens. I jump off the front of the vehicle and go over to the Iraqi, showing off my best cowboy-American-Marine swagger. *Speak English dear God let him speak English.* I greet him in Arabic.

"Salaam Alaikum." I must have an accent, something makes him laugh.

"Alaikum Salaam."

"Speak English?"

"A little." *Yes!*

"I'm Jeff"

"Ahkmed"

"Nice to meet you." We grip hands tight and resist letting go just long enough so as not to get busted. We exchange small talk as much as possible for a few minutes and I begin to wonder if . . . I don't know, I want more. There's no way we can do anything, but I'm desperate for at a verbal acknowledgment of what we both know. He figures out how.

"You have wife?" he asks me.

"No. No wife. You?"

"No wife," he answers, and then his beautiful brown eyes lit up. I'm a sucker for brown eyes. "Why?" he says again, flirting. I just smile. We're making out big-time with our words. "You're beautiful," he says quietly as his eyes dart around to make sure no one hears.

"Yeah, you're beautiful too." You can see the electricity in the air between us, and my cammie bottoms are getting tighter by the second. I think he's having the same problem. We stand there enjoying the torture of our situation.

"You have . . ." And he pantomimes "lip balm." I dig in my pocket and produce my dirty, half-used tube. I gotta tell you, I don't think anyone's ever put on lip balm in a sexier way. "What you call . . ." And he kisses the air.

"What's this?" I ask and make the kissing noise.

"Yes"

"Kiss. We call it kiss."

"Kiss," he repeats and hands back the ChapStick.

"No, no. You keep it." I put up my hand to refuse it.

"Kiss," he repeats and pushes it into my palm. *Well I'll be damned, he's giving me a kiss.* I smooth the stuff onto my own lips as he watches, and in an instant my anger at both our cultures' ignorance is diminished, and shame and anger are overcome by bliss and absolute pride—in us, in our people, in our everlasting overcoming, in our ability to love, to show love no matter what. We are everywhere. We are Love and we shall overcome.

"Hey Key, let's roll, dawg." *Fuck.*

"Good-bye Ahkmed." And I slap the lip balm back into his palm. "Kiss."

"Good-bye Jeff."

I leap onto my vehicle with my best cowboy-American-Marine-jumping-on-his horse leap. He sadly smiles but with a dose of gratitude and acceptance as I pull on my comm helmet and try madly to impress him as I fire up the LAV and prepare to roll. As we leave, I look back one more time as he walks toward his house. This time he does not look back.

I grew up in very rural Alabama, so my gaydar is a very fine-tuned instrument. During my brief stay in the Middle East, I would see them there, in the crowd, on the street, in the market...those Iraqi versions of me, trying their best to get along in a horrible situation. When a man finds himself a part of something like war, he *must* let himself believe that he is there for a good reason. When our eyes would meet and that whatever it is that happens would happen, so much would happen in just that split second. The volumes of communication that can occur in a nanosecond is an unbelievable phenomenon. Perhaps it is a survival mechanism given to our "tribe" by the creator. In that instant I would think, *Maybe your life as a gay man will be better now, my brother.* His eyes would say, "Tell me what it is like to walk in the market and hold hands with the man you love." (I would hate for him to know that is an experience known only to certain city-dwellers in America, and that those days seem to be slipping away as the climate of fascism in America heats up degrees by the second.) There would be hope in his eyes, hope for a better life. As more and more is revealed about the real reasons the Bush Administration sent us to Iraq, and as global approval of America's foreign policy plummets by the day, one wonders how long it will be safe for Americans to travel abroad at all, much less to a Muslim country. Only time will answer this question. I know one thing for sure, not one day goes by that I do not think of my Iraqi soccer player and wonder if he lived . . . and of all my fellow Marines, so many of them gay, serving silently in a war that never should have been.

# Winter, 1995

*Don Bapst*

You arrived in a taxi from hell with no shocks or seat belt, weaving in and out of the violent cauldron of cars—some scraping the guard-rails at sixty mph plus on a pothole-ridden excuse for a road. If your driver stopped abruptly, you'd be under those wheels in seconds flat. But you never stopped.

Cairo. A dusty, colonial-era hotel off Midan Tahrir with a cob-webbed chandelier and a wooden elevator from the 1930s. Sheikhs smoking *shisha* in luxury hotels. Men with black teeth and dusty robes diving onto moving buses. Women hiding under billowing silk scarves, toting children behind their husbands. Donkeys towing pre-carious cartloads of fruit through unfiltered traffic. Islamic mosques and Coptic churches, plastic pyramids and papyrus Qurans. Men bending over prayer mats in the street. Women weeping over Chris-tian reliquary.

You had no idea where you were. Strands of colored lights draped from Oriental buildings flashed by the windows, and you prayed your driver was taking you to the hotel you'd told him about and not into some deserted alley to take your luggage and your life in the name of Allah or hunger or both.

He had to ask directions from about five locals and drove in what seemed like (and probably were) circles. But you got to your hotel. He tried to raise the price he'd quoted. You paid more than the going rate, but less than he'd asked for. He protested exactly three times in a red-faced rage, then thanked you warmly, kissing the bills and offer-ing them to Allah before pocketing them and driving off. This was less dangerous than New York you figured when you finally closed the door on the swirl of new information, but it was a danger that you

*Gay Travels in the Muslim World*
© 2007 by The Haworth Press, Inc. All rights reserved.
doi:10.1300/5481_09

didn't know how to interpret, and so it was more threatening. What were people capable of here? Less? More? The same as "back home?"

\* \* \*

A man with a broken leg and a rickety crutch hobbled over to me from the exact opposite corner of the mosque, just as prayers were beginning to resonate through the mystical space: "Aaaallllaaaahhh!"
"Crypt. I show you crypt."
"No thank you. *Shukran.*"
He limped back over the prayer mats, his disfigured right foot flopping in the dusty air, probably broken by his father when he was a kid so he'd bring in more cash when they went out begging together. I should have gone to look at his crypt or mausoleum or whatever the fuck it was. He'd made that difficult trajectory just for me. A path he wouldn't have taken had I stayed in Paris or the United States. A path determined largely by my presence there.
"Hey, Amir. How much did that guy give you for the crypt tour?"
"Are you kidding! He wouldn't even look at it."
"What? Those Americans are so damn stingy."
"Ain't that the truth. They're just here to see the pyramids and maybe a mosque or two, then it's back on the tour bus . . ."
Some of those guys had probably worked in the same mosque—checking peoples' shoes, showing off the crypt, turning on and off the lights, sweeping the floors, shaking the rugs—for years, maybe decades. They'd probably continue to do it for decades to come. And for one day I was not only an observer of their daily drama, but a flesh-and-blood thing-to-be-dealt-with—plunged into their midst without warning or apology. We interacted through a series of rapid gestures, intricate expressions, a few English words and even fewer Arabic ones, all before my hasty departure. I was to their career in that mosque what the late twentieth century is to the whole of Egyptian history: a flash in the dark—a split second.
But by being there, in the midst of people as real and complicated as me, I exposed them to my essence as I absorbed theirs. I proposed

my reality by putting it, undeniably, in their faces, as I succumbed to their reality, surrounding myself with it, falling into it.

\* \* \*

To the whole staff of the Metropolitan Hotel:

Thank you for making our time in Cairo a special one. We will never forget the warm welcome we received from all of you. A special thanks goes to Naguib, who drove us to Saqqara and Giza, and to Amir, who drove us to Al-Fayoum. (We hope that they are able to fix your car, Amir!)

We were extremely touched by the warmth and kindness of all the Egyptian people, and we are recommending to all our friends that they cancel their vacation plans and go instead to Egypt! We are sure they won't be disappointed.

And so, till we find the way to make another voyage to Cairo: *Shukran* and *Salaam!*

\* \* \*

The eyes of Islamic Cairo are on the back of your head as you walk through its poorest streets with your American sneakers and your French traveler's checks. You stand in the dirt of a neighborhood where the language being chanted from the minarets is a language you can't even begin to understand—a language that is perhaps most beautiful when it spells out its darkest threats and curses and that spits when it tries to be tender. Tears are cried for different reasons here, and familiar gestures mean something else—something older than the name of the country where you happened to be born.

Allah . . . There was something to that word that made sense in these gorgeous streets, shrouded in the luxury of silky dust.

O People of the Scripture! Do not exaggerate in your religion or utter aught concerning Allah save the truth.

The people of this city went to work, hardly complaining. Who were the terrorists? What percentage of these shuffling masses? I took off my shoes and I smelled the incense in the massive mosques. Here in Egypt, the ruins hadn't been restored, and they were all the more beautiful for it. Violence lurked under the surface as it lurks in any city. But the real miracle was that these sixteen million people, balanced near the edge of collapse (just like the people of New York, Paris, Bangkok, New Delhi, Chicago, and Mexico), didn't fall upon one another. The city functioned as it had for centuries, weaving in and out of itself in an intricate fluctuation of flesh and machinery. The women pushing through the crowd with their scarves and baskets had work to do. So did the men with their carts of sand and fruit. "Coming through! Out of the way!" Life went on and on.

And that was also the tragedy: that the people of Cairo hadn't all become terrorists, protesting against the poverty that they'd been taught to passively accept, that they continued giving birth to children they could barely feed, that they never questioned their placement among these crumbling Cairo stones.

*   *   *

Letter to the Metropolitan Hotel, translated into French by the computer:

*Au personnel entier de l'Hôtel Metropolite:*

*Merci pour fabrication notre temps au Caire un on spécial. Nous oublierons jamais le chaud bienvenu nous avons reçu de tout de vous. Un remerciements spéciaux vont à Naguib, qui nous a conduits à Saqqara et Giza, et à Amir, qui nous a conduits à Al-Fayoum. (Nous espérons qu'ils sont capable d'arranger votre voiture, Amir!)*

*Nous étions extrêmement a touché par la chaleur et gentillesse de toutes les personnes du Égyptien, et nous recommandons à tous nos amis qui ils annulent leurs vacances organisent et aller au lieu en Égypte! Nous sommes sûrs ils ne seront pas déçus.*

*Et donc, jusqu'à ce que nous trouvons le chemin faire le voyage un autre au Caire : Shukran et Salaam!*

\*   \*   \*

Back in Paris, French Front Nationalist Nazi Le Pen had managed to get more than 16 percent of France (more than 5 million people!) to support his violently racist agenda. In France, this was not considered fundamentalism or terrorism, it was considered an "unfortunate" reaction to the fundamentalism of other countries and its effect on French unemployment. What percentage of Egyptians had declared such a systematic war against its foreigners? Sixteen percent? Less? More? And how many supporters had the latest American nationalist managed to drum up? Were people even slightly less stupid anywhere in the world?

\*   \*   \*

"Where you from?"

We had quickly tired of answering that question, inevitably followed up by an unwanted visit to the nearest papyrus shop or an aggressive offer of a taxi to the pyramids. This time it was a persistent teenager. "Welcome in Egypt. Where you from?"

To respond "Franc," was a lot easier than, "I'm American and he's German, but we live in France, which is why we're speaking French."

"Oh, you French think you something really special."

"Well, some do."

"You like Egypt?"

"Yes."

"Many tourists stop coming from France, from Germany, from America, but it's good, no? *Très bon,* eh?"

"They're scared because they heard about terrorism . . ."

"No! No terrorism! No problem. Egypt good. Many tourists. No problem. These are things television say to bring shame on Egypt. They make us look bad."

"Well, we find the Egyptians very kind; we've had no problems at all."

"Why don't you come and look my shop? I show you papyrus for good price."

"No thank you. We don't need any papyrus today."

"But I make you good price! Just look."

"No, really."

"You take my card. Just come with me to my car and I give it you."

"No, *really*. Thank you. *Shukran*."

What were we to these people besides a wallet full of dollars? Did they understand what our money was worth to us back in our rich countries? Did they know of the poverty in Chicago, Paris, New York, Berlin? Did they understand any better than we did the reasons why a thing called a stock market made one currency "stronger" than another? And, by the way, did that flirtatious gleam in their eyes mean they knew we were fags who fucked each other back in our hotel room? Did the concept of homosexuality even exist in their language? Did the guys walking down the street with their arms intertwined make love when girls weren't available? Were some of the guys who stopped us in the street looking for sex with us too? Did they exchange sex for money? Did they believe that they would go to hell for it? Did they care? Did they believe in their religion as much as a Baptist in Harlem believes in his Sunday school or a Catholic from my hometown believes in the Pope's interpretation of the Bible?

Was there really less freedom in Muslim Egypt than in a country like France or the United States, where you had "the freedom to be who you wanted to be" provided you had the money to escape from your small town to disappear into a big city's lonely ghetto?

Those were questions based on the references of my life, references that were practically insignificant here in Egypt where English was the language of authority, money, and tourism, but not communication; where Western media was edited by authorities of the oldest university in the world; and where people found a way, nevertheless, to interact—physically, emotionally, even vibrantly—without the values, categories, religion, or culture of the part of the world where I came from.

*    *    *

Letter to the Metropolitan Hotel, translated back from the French by the same computer:

To the whole personnel of the Metropolitan hotel:

Thank you for manufacture our time to the Cairo an one special. We will ever forget the hot welcome us received of all of you. A special acknowledgements go to Naguib, who conducted Saqqara us and Giza, and to Amir, who conducted us to Al-Fayoum. (We hope that they are capable of arranging your car, Amir!)

We were extremely touched by the heat and niceness of all the persons of Egyptian, and we recommend to all our friends who they nullify their vacations organizes and go to the place in Egypt! We are sure they won't be disappointed.

And therefore, until is the path make the trip an other to the Cairo: *Shukran* and *Salaam!*

\*   \*   \*

Farmers worked the irrigated banks of the Nile as their ancestors had done for fifty centuries, maybe longer. People used too much sugar, smoked too many cigarettes, let their teeth rot. The vertebrae scattered among the pebbles were human vertebrae, mixed with shreds of pharaonic pottery. Everything flaked away into the same desert dust—bowls, jars, houses, stones, and the bones of the people who'd shaped them all—just as all the religious texts ever written had promised they would. Eventually, the texts themselves would disintegrate, along with the rest of earthly matter. The only thing we knew for certain about our destinies was down there in the sand.

I was standing on the base of the Great Pyramid as millions of other people had done for dozens of centuries.

Back in San Francisco, Dan was probably taking his AZT pills, or maybe he'd given them up entirely. He was lying, perhaps, in the arms of his lover Mike, or maybe in the arms of someone else, or maybe between two men at the same time as Dan and I once lay together with Thomas on the floor of our Jones Street apartment, touching each other slowly and wondering at the contents of each other's infinite eyes. Who paid the rent on that apartment now? And where was Thomas? I'd last bumped into him in the center of the crowd in Central Park at Stonewall 25, and his lips had tasted so good when I kissed him hello . . . What did Stonewall mean to those Egyptians pounding on those old rocks down there?

A man in a long, gray robe blew a whistle and told me to get down. "No climb." I hadn't made it up more than a few steps, but, anyway, that was enough for me. What I really wanted to know was just what did they wear under their robes? I would have loved to ask him, but a camel was making its way toward us.

"You take camel?"

"I don't like camels."

"I give you good price."

"No."

"Do you know the price?"

"Don't want. No camel. Camel bad."

Was Dan a symbol like this camel was a symbol? When a tour bus rolled down Castro Street, did the people inside snap a picture of him holding his boyfriend's hand? Would he be featured on some TV documentary as an AIDS victim? Was he already playing that role in my mind? Was Dan "My Sick Friend Back in the States who Needs Me"? Could anyone so far away be anything more specific to me than a symbol?

"This good camel. Nice camel."

It was a nice camel. It was cleaner than the others I'd seen, and it didn't have that nasty smirk on its lips like so many other bad examples.

"Yes, nice camel. No money." I pulled out the bare lining of my pocket. The camel moved away. Where did these camel guys come from, anyway? Had their ancestors been in the business for centuries, selling rides to Greek and Roman tourists long before the birth of Christ?

\*　　\*　　\*

We met Hassan when Naguib, our taxi driver, dropped us off at the door of a horse and camel stable and turned us over to him. We turned down the animals at once, but there didn't seem to be any way of turning down Hassan: "This is Sphinx. Some persons say Napoleon broke nose, some say . . ." We knew all that and much more than he could possibly explain to us in his limited if functional English, but without getting downright nasty, there was no choice but to let him go on.

I decided I'd try changing the subject as often as possible to see just how much about "the real Cairo" I could pump out of him in the two hours the universe had allotted us together.

"What do the pyramids mean to the Egyptian people?"

"Some think they are not more than pile of stones. But I see them sometimes, and I think I see them for the first time. When I see them this way, they don't look to be rocks."

"No, they look soft. Like a sponge."

"Yes."

Paul took our picture from a nearby hill, where another tourist camel was bearing down on him. "Picture, picture?"

"I dreamed of coming to see the pyramids since I was a small child," I told Hassan, "but I had no idea then that the Muslim culture was every bit as fascinating as the pharaonic one or that I'd be visiting as many ancient mosques in Egypt as pyramids and tombs."

"What do you think of Islamic religion? Many tourists think it is only terrorists and bad things."

"Well, we only hear about the terrorists at home, and not about the good points."

I watched him cringe, like I was stating my opinion and not the one I'd heard about. If only I'd had a few years of Arabic so I could be the one butchering a language. It's much less dangerous to search for basic words than to simplify complicated sentences. "From what I've already seen in my first days here, Muslims seem to be good people." American clichés are always a safe bet when dealing with people who barely speak English, since they usually provide just the touch of flattery required.

Hassan told me he was studying Islamic religion at Cairo University where he had to fight with the rich kids for the best seats in class. He drank and "had a girlfriend"—which seemed to mean he had an active sexual partner—though through his own interpretation of the Quran, both were forbidden.

"You have to live!" He wanted to go to New Zealand one day because he had another girlfriend who lived there. "Egyptians like to fuck too much."

Hassan said the worst tourists were the English, followed by the French. The Japanese were fascinated by everything they saw, he said, and they nodded vigorously at his English commentary, but when he asked them, "Do you understand?" they didn't even understand the word "understand."

American soldiers were Hassan's favorites. They liked camel rides, and they tipped accordingly. They talked about the babes they'd fucked at rowdy beer bashes back home—stuff that seemed like freedom to a financially restricted young Egyptian.

Hassan was working his way through college by forcing his tour guide services onto people like them, people like me. People who came from all over the world to see the pyramids and who found themselves led around the desert by a Muslim in a dusty robe.

On a nearby hill, three Australian girls formed a pyramid with their bodies. One lay on the ground as the base, the others leaned over her, giggling, to make the sides. Their Egyptian guide, who spoke English with the accent and expressions of an American jock, took their picture with the Great Pyramid off in the distance—fitting it snugly inside the frame formed by their bodies. "Oh, that's gonna be a good picture!" They all got back on their camels and rode off laughing.

The universe had put us together like that on a dreamy desert stage, Hassan and me and Paul and the Australians in the distance, to act out our pathetic human drama. We'd come to that spot—me, the giddy Australians, the stuffy Brits, the arrogant French, the trashy Americans, the showy Saudi Arabians, the orderly Japanese, the vulgar Italians—as people had for centuries: to contemplate our own deaths. The pyramids had, after all, been built as an escape from the inevitable, and people the world over wanted to see how the greatest masterpiece in the history of the world had failed. How many stones would it take to actually reach heaven if these enormous structures weren't enough? What kind of burial chamber would be impervious to thieves and decay?

Hassan took us back to the taxi, and we gave him fifty Egyptian pounds. "Oh, that's really nothing, you know for several hours with private guide. I must pay the stable, and I must pay my school . . ." We finished with sixty.

"You happy?"

"It's just that, well, it seems that you're only interested in what kind of money I can give you."

"No, you must not give me something if you not happy. Are you happy?"

"Well . . ." It was only a couple bucks more than the price any guidebook said was correct, but he'd have obviously worked me for whatever he thought I'd fork out, like I was just another one of "those foreigners" with a pocket full of money. Not exactly the basis for an equitable, friendly understanding. But what did I really understand about what that currency meant to Hassan?

"Okay. Yes, I'm happy."

"Okay."

With a little prying, we learned that Naguib got a discount on parking rates by introducing us to Hassan. Hassan got a cut from whatever we might have paid to the horse and camel people too. Since we went beastless, he'd have to fork over some of what we gave him to the stable. Or so he told us. It's not like we could go verify any of this with any sort of better business bureau. The tourist police dotting the landscape were there to stop blatant violence. This was much more subtle, much harder to escape. Money took on such a different meaning that it lost all meaning. I didn't care so much that I was parting with mine. I just wanted to understand why I was parting with it and who was going to get it in the end. But who dares argue about economics with the direct descendants of the people who created civilization?

\*   \*   \*

Baksheesh line:

Tracing each of the three hundred American dollars that I converted and spent during my eight days in Egypt—the exact path of each fraction of each cent right down to the names, professions, and annual incomes of the people who finally pocketed my piastres.

\*    \*    \*

If it was tempting to get all mystical and romantic about standing on the actual site of the birth of society, it was important to remember that this is where the problems had begun, and where none had ever been resolved.

There was a nightly light show at the pyramids: thirty pounds to get in. The Arabic prayer music from a nearby ghetto battled with the soundtrack to *Cleopatra* for our attention.

"The pyramids are the greatest achievement ever accomplished by man!" boomed the speakers.

Which, sadly enough, was more or less true, meaning that the last fifty centuries or so of history had done nothing but create a little laser technology for this tacky, corporate-sponsored, energy-wasting, tourist spectacle. When the Sphinx changed from blue to red then back to yellow, all the flashes in the crowd went off in a burst of "oohs" and "aahs." *This would be exactly where I'd plant my bomb if I were a terrorist,* I thought. Spare the pyramids and the residents of Giza, but don't leave a single tourist standing, not even me.

\*    \*    \*

Paul left me in the hotel one night to go and smoke *shisha*. In the street he met Ihab. "Where you from? Ah, so! *Deutschland! Gut!*"

They went to a café and talked about Germany. What kind of beer did they serve in Germany? How much did an average German family make? How had their currency gotten so much stronger? How did you say *shisha* in German? Were German girls really easier? Could he borrow twenty Egyptian pounds till later?

Paul came back to the hotel after they promised to see each other again. Ihab wanted to meet me too. I said I didn't want to. I wasn't interested in discussing American business, girls, films, and money. Paul said I was being closed-minded. I agreed. Closed-minded meant not letting in any old piece of information into my already overloaded receptor. That seemed sensible behavior given our eight-day status as Western tourists in a third world country. We didn't understand Arab culture well enough to know what kind of problems we could expect when it was discovered we were a same-sex couple. I didn't want to explore questions such as, "Where do you guys live?" "Where do you work?" and "How many girlfriends do you have?" till I knew more about what answering them meant.

I knew I was being a coward, but I was only willing to be courageous if I had the intention of investing more than a week in this experience. Explaining our same-sex relationship to an Egyptian would take months, not minutes. And how could we really develop any sort of genuine communication with someone while hiding that essential aspect of our lives? It seemed impossible to make even the most distant reference to homosexuality when the Egyptian censors had removed all suggestion of it from books and films, on the grounds that it was the primary offense against God, at least according to the most popular reading of the Quran. Queers undoubtedly existed in Egypt, even without Western references, but in what form? As a statue of Akhenaton, the Drag Queen Pharaoh, back in the Egyptian Museum? As a quick, premarital fuck in a hammam? As a warped, Western eccentricity brought about by an extravagant capitalist lifestyle? It would take time to learn how to communicate about such things. We'd have to find a new vocabulary. Hell, we'd have to learn Arabic for starters. I was sure it was all possible, but it would take more time than we were allowing ourselves on this visit.

Paul went out with Ihab a couple of times while I stayed at the hotel watching Arabic television.

"I need to fuck at *least* once a day," he proudly confided in Paul. He liked to party. I told Paul that I wouldn't be tempted to spend my free time hanging out with a party-hardy guy whether he was Egyptian, German, Dutch, or American. Paul thought he was really diving into the local life or something. He didn't seem to be bothered that Ihab was probably known by locals as the guy who lured in tourists with his English skills, working them for a couple of pounds or a piece of pussy or maybe even a piece of ass.

On our last night, Ihab insisted on coming with us to the airport. Muslims were not allowed to buy alcohol in stores since it was against their religion, but we could buy it and pass it on to him. "Don't worry, guy, I have money!"

*O ye who believe! Strong drink and games of chance and idols are only an infamy of Satan's handiwork. Leave it aside in order that ye may succeed.*

"We can't leave the airport once we've passed through security," I pointed out.

"Yes, yes! No problem."

Paul was already agreeing.

"Well, if you want to do it, Paul, you can, but I feel really uncomfortable about it. First of all, I don't like to mess around with airport security. Second, I feel that when I'm in another country I should respect the local culture."

"But it's just for the party. You know, 'Party, party!'"

Dude.

"I'm not sure that not having alcohol is one of Egypt's biggest problems. In fact, I think even we'd be much better off without it." I was getting fed up with the horny teen. If it weren't for the Egyptian accent I'd have sworn he'd graduated from my high school.

*Satan seeketh only to cast among you enmity and hatred by means of strong drink and games of chance, and to turn you from remembrance of Allah and from worship.*

"Anyway, Ihab, I'm not going to be the bad Western tourist who exports what is considered by many to be 'evil' into a culture that has been functioning just fine without it for quite some time."

Paul changed his mind once I put it that way. "Yes, I think we must think of your customs here. You told me before that you follow some of Islamic teachings but not others, so I don't know really which are important because I am not Muslim."

"Okay, okay. So let's just forget it," he said without a touch of irony, having already forgotten the idea, it seemed.

*Say: The evil and the good are not alike even though the plenty of the evil attract thee. So be mindful of your duty to Allah, O men of understanding, that ye may succeed.*

He still wanted to come with us to the airport. I was sure this was going to turn into a final plea for the booze or something worse. He was probably the fundamentalist of our nightmares, plotting an airport action with me in the starring role of First Victim.

He hopped in the front with our driver, Amir. We sailed past the Islamic colors of Cairo, making the same trajectory we'd made the night of our arrival, only in reverse. Those strings of Christmas lights hanging off the minarets and mosques were illuminating places we knew and had been to. Some of them had names and stories. They were a part of our lives. We knew when we passed through one neighborhood and into another and when the taxi was going in the right direction. We were saying good-bye to a city we'd lived in for slightly more than a mere moment of our lives.

The taxi arrived suddenly, not feeling like a taxi anymore, but like Amir's car.

Well, like Amir's cousin's car. Amir's car was getting repaired somewhere outside Giza since it had broken down two nights before on our way back from Al-Fayoum. He'd flagged down a turbaned guy in a truck who kindly hauled us forty kilometers through the desert with nothing but a tattered old rope tied to his bumper.

Amir jumped out at the airport entrance with tears in his eyes. He hugged us both, kissed us on the cheeks. Ihab too. The alcohol project was long forgotten. They were both gushing with sentimental tears, severely exaggerating the importance we'd held in each others' lives. It was a sentimentality only exacerbated by the technology and capital that had allowed us to whip in and out of their country in a matter of days to form such instant relationships, only to break them off before they could reach their infancy. We all indulged in the sweet sadness. Soon we were dragging our bags into the airport as they drove off—before any of the absurd fears on either side of the culture gap could be realized.

But what exactly had we meant to them?

# ❧ 10    Love, Sex, and Religion:
Betrayed in Muslim Morocco

*Richard Ammon*

## A Gracious Man and a Fatal Mistake

My friend George was murdered in Morocco, stabbed multiple times by an enraged assailant who escaped the scene immediately after. Three weeks later the police captured the culprit, a young Arab Muslim man who was wearing George's ring and had his wallet in a back pocket. The motive, said the police, was robbery. I doubt it.

Closer to the truth, I think, was that George hadn't fulfilled his part of a "deal" with Mustapha, his killer. The deal didn't involve drugs or contraband or simply money, despite the robbery face police put on the killing. No, the deal was more subtle, more layered. It had to do with "sex and consequences," and George made the mistake of overlooking that for a moment.

An educated American from California, a teacher, a film and theater critic, and a writer, George was well-known and respected in London and El Jadida, an ancient town on Morocco's Atlantic west coast. He moved to Morocco about eleven years ago, as had many European and American artists and writers throughout the twentieth century (Baron von Gloeden, Oscar Wilde, and André Gide, Paul Bowles and Jane Auer among them), after succumbing to the ambisexual mystique that seethed in the beautiful dark eyes of younger Arab men. The Encyclopedia of Gay, Lesbian, Bisexual, Transgender, and Queer Culture (www.glbtq.com) said of the famous Polish classical composer Carl Szymanowski that after his first visit, "he found the

*Gay Travels in the Muslim World*
© 2007 by The Haworth Press, Inc. All rights reserved.
doi:10.1300/5481_10

uninhibited southern climate to be psychologically liberating and, thereby, an inspiration to his life and work as an artist."

Romantic, sunny, sensual, mysterious, and clandestine—North Africa's secrets have swayed the minds of countless men from the north and the west for centuries. Whether artist or merchant; whether for sex or love, for inspiration or solitude, for the jumble of the medina scents or the endless sands, life in Muslim Arab Africa for "outcast" men (as Wilde called himself) is the antidote to pale-skin puritan life.

For innumerable lesser-known men who today wander to the southern shores of the Mediterranean, this same allure continues, unchanged, like the phases of the moon: poor but handsome Muslim men and boys willing to offer themselves to the fantasy lullabies of foreigners in exchange for their own dreams of money or escape.

And this is where the danger lurks.

George knew well the arrangement, but he did not know Mustapha well enough, it had been less than a year. A few previous relationships had turned out well as George served as mentor, godfather, financial contributor, personal advisor, education provider, or job finder in return for the occasional sweet affections of his protégés. When it came time, inevitably, for the young man to marry, George became the friendly "uncle" and was received as part of the family. So it had been for many years, and George was a contented man, with friends and loved ones. With Mustapha, aged twenty-four, another young life was being nurtured and advanced by George, balanced by the younger man's compliance. What went wrong?

### Arranged Matches

Sex between strangers is fragile and unpredictable. Sometimes it's true love, sometimes a five-minute trick, and other times it is a bargain, a deal—not a gift of pleasure or expression of feelings.

George was very aware of this and didn't get lost in his own emotions for his paramours. For his part, he returned much more than he received. In exchange for an occasional night together the swarthy younger one had his life changed from an impoverished, unskilled manual or unemployed worker to an educated employee with marketable abilities. Over time, a warm attachment formed between the two men even after the obligatory wife entered the picture.

Such was the arrangement with strikingly handsome Mustapha with the hazel eyes and who aspired to be an actor. To his mind, no doubt, George was his ticket to fame and wealth since George had friends and acquaintances in the starry world of film and theater. Most likely, there were candlelight conversations between them in which visions and dreams were voiced but without promises. George knew better than to promise the moon. We can't know what George really said or what Mustapha expected, but over time Mustapha's imagination collided with the reality of George's limits. He could not put Mustapha's name in lights. An argument ensued, voices were raised, fury overtook Mustapha, and steel flashed. In the end, Mustapha took what he could—a few items, including some money.

### Risky Liaisons

I tell this sad tale to make a tragic point: beyond being fragile and unpredictable, sex between some Arabs and Muslims and foreigners—in this case an experienced and "self-identified gay man" who knew what gay love was—can sometimes be "fatal." George paid with his life, but more often it's the heart that suffers.

For some in the Arabic world, the Muslim religion and culture is toxic to nonmarital sex, toxic to men who have sex with men (and women with women), toxic to those who love others of their own gender. It is toxic to the truth of sexual attraction.

And it's hypocritical: across the vast spread of Muslim masculinity, from Morocco to India, it is well known that premarital young men have sex with one another since women are mostly forbidden to them. A woman's virginity is a badge of family honor at the time of her marriage.

It's also well known that such widespread homo-sex is vehemently denied and defended against in public. Absurd displays of "justice" against the "abomination" include toppling walls, stoning to death, beheading, or imprisonment. Much more common are punishing glares and cold shoulders that induce shame and guilt. Rejection from families is perhaps the worst penalty. By such cruelty, it is alleged, the purity of Islamic law and Arab cultural norms are self-righteously maintained.

Such killing, maiming, jailing, or discarding of men for the acts of homosexual pleasure or love is a profound violation of human nature and social justice. Equally profound, such enmity defiles the gay spirit that strives to live in the hearts of LGBT Muslims worldwide. On gay Muslim chat sites men and women express anguish, guilt, shame, and much fear of family discovery. (I don't for a moment suggest that certain LGBT Christians or Jews don't experience equal anguish.) The astringent prohibitions of Islam on the naturalness, tenderness, and truthfulness of gay love and same-sex desire are heartless. Countless LGBT Muslims live in high anxiety and dark closets, ashamed of their inner truth. It is very difficult for them to transcend this bog of fear and loathing.

## A Caveat

It's always difficult to delineate the behavior of a minority of people without unintentionally imposing on the reality of others. In contrast to the forbidding description of Muslim sexuality here, this writer is very aware of the "progressive" Muslim movement currently gaining momentum in numerous countries. As considerate Muslim devotees, they reject homophobia and anti-Semitism. They are pro-choice and urge equality among genders. Among these open-minded Muslims are genuinely loving gay and lesbian couples and singles (virtually invisible to outsiders). I do not refer to them here. I also do not refer to men who enjoy casual gay sex with no exchange of money; there are many bisexual Muslim men who are prosperous and would be insulted if money were part of the moment. Nor do I refer to genuinely gay Muslims who need to sell sex with other men as a means of support. At least they are being honest about their desire even if their motives are mercenary. No, I refer here to another sort of sexual creature.

## Star-Crossed Haters

Out of the quagmire of doubled-crossed sexual feelings and cash schemes comes an unwelcome player—a nongay Muslim man who cruises gay non-Muslim men using deceptive homosexual behavior. An impoverished and probably love-starved native, hostile to gay sex, uses it to entice and abuse queer men's sincere desire for intimacy. Gay sex for sale by a straight man. A liar selling lies.

Was Mustapha really gay or one of these pretenders? I suspect he was both. By killing George was he trying to kill his own homosexual impulses? Was he seeking revenge against his own absent father who preferred to spend time with other men smoking in a café than with his family? Such questions now seem moot, now that both lives have been lost.

Mustapha, very likely, was raised to disgust homosexuality, but was driven to it by his own sex drive and a craving for money. It's not likely the young man fully desired George (in his sixties) to be his lover, but he was certainly a benign father figure as well as an appealing wallet and ticket out of the country—strong enough motives for Mustapha to keep George in his sights and "put out" on occasion. Mustapha's affectations toward George were sincere enough to lull George into forgetting, over time, to be watchful, until the youth proved his truth. George was lulled into forgetting what the deal really was, exposing his very real Achilles' heel for male beauty. In hindsight, George didn't stand a chance against this pretty boy with foul motives.

## Foolish Liaison

My own brush with the antagonism that lies beneath such encounters was far less hazardous than George's. A friend and I were cruised one evening after dinner as we walked along the harbor in Essaouria. It was less of a cruise than it was verbal badgering by two young natives very intent on taking us back to their place for "what you like." Their insistent chatter was about sex, about their being students, about how we liked Morocco, and about more sex—the usual clap that passes for talk between people who do not know or trust one another. The young cruisers were pleasant looking enough to be acceptable. Their words were erotic and seductive. My friend and I are not tightly prudish (although usually cautious), and we allow low-risk adventure as part of our travels.

We let ourselves be led to the home of one of the guys who sneaked us into a ground-floor room; his nervousness about keeping very quiet made us uneasy. I presumed his family was asleep in the other rooms. In the dark, we fumbled around and felt body parts until the sleaziness of the situation (and the realization that these guys were probably not homosexual) finally flattened any desire we might have had. We got dressed (did we undress at all?) and we headed out into the warm night air and the dim street. They wanted money of course, as we expected.

Since we hadn't anticipated this pickup we had little cash on us. We gave them most of what we had, which obviously wasn't enough—not what they expected from two white tourists (although it was probably more than they could make for a week's labor in a shop). Upset and argumentative, they pressed us to go back and get more money from our hotel room. We argued back that no price had been set and we had no more money in our pockets. They followed us, bickering and complaining, but held back as we approached the entrance of our hotel and the manager came out to greet us. He immediately sensed the situation and shouted at the kids to go away as he ushered us inside. (Later, in private, we learned from the manager—married with kids—that he had had a twenty-five year relationship with an Englishman.)

More than relieved we felt foolish at ourselves for getting into that situation. Although a little nervous, we had not been too worried as we were both bigger than they were. It didn't occur to us that they might have had a weapon—even more foolish. The unfriendly exchange reminded me—again—of the risk in the lure of sex from enticing figures, and it reawakened my awareness of the edgy, insincere, hormone-and-money-driven motives that drive these young men to offer phony sex to pale-faced visitors.

## *Betrayal of Homosexuality*

Thinking back on that night and other seductive attempts by natives (it happened four times during a visit to Morocco and several times in Egypt) and thinking about George, I feel an unexpected sense of resentment toward these street seducers. I know I should feel some sympathy for their plight (which I do, to a degree, and as I'm sure George did) but they commit an offense—and are no doubt unaware of it.

For more than a generation we in the West have fought (and died) to gain recognition and validation of our form of same-sex life and love. In the twenty-first century, it is still an uphill battle against bigotry, as recent antigay marriage amendments that passed in a dozen states in America will testify.

Love and its close affiliate sexual arousal (gay or straight) are both highly vulnerable states of being that, between two respectful adults, should be treated with mutual respect and satisfying responses. I realize of course that often it's not. Over my lifetime, living by accident within a highly developed LGBT culture, I know the truth and profoundness of my homosexually oriented love and erotic desires. I have developed dignity and appreciation for my own queer feelings and for those of my LGBT brothers and sisters who move through similar sentient states. Many modern queer folks subscribe to this affirmation and a healthy subcultural "norm" guides our behavior and anticipates others' behavior: gay love is authentic and is to be prized.

## *Foreign Territory*

A disconnect exists, an emotional (or at least a social) risk that sometimes awaits the foreign visitor when he lands on Muslim Arab soil. Like dangling fake diamonds before a jeweler, countless appealing Arab boys and young men have become adept at proffering their sexuality to outsiders, using phony homosexuality to seduce, steal, or coax money from unsuspecting—or suspicious but vulnerable—non-Arab homosexual men.

Such faux homosexual behavior is offensive to what we have worked hard to validate. These are straight homophobes abusing gay men with deceptive sexuality. Sex with other men for them is a crass bargain without affection. They offer (mostly feeble) genital manipulation and demand dollars in return. What should be an intimate, mutual give-and-take exchange is shot through with hypocrisy, lying, and pretense.

I realize much the same can be said about prostitution in general, across thousands of years and hundreds of cultures, but I think there is a difference between heterosexual and homosexual passion for sale and who's peddling it. The vast majority of "sellers" are hetero women (and some men) who seduce other hetero johns (or janes) for "acceptable" sex. At least they are truthful to their sexual orientation.

But a whole cadre of hetero Muslim men engage in what they feel is forbidden sex, betraying themselves as well as homo men's desire. They are contemptuous of gay men's vulnerabilities, abusing our affections with hollow affectations that can turn quickly into hostility when the price is not right.

Whatever the details of George's demise, I believe he was betrayed by a tormented young soul lost in the cross-currents of his own poverty, sexual desire, and religious dogma.

## ও 11

# Work In Progress:
# Notes from a Continuing Journey
# of Manufacturing Dissent

*Parvez Sharma*

Paris, January 2004, 9:28 pm

We sit, the three of us, at Le Depot, a sex club not too far from the Marais. The air is thick with the smell of sweat and cum. Lithe French boys walk around, hard, hungry, and white. They look at our brownness with primal need in their eyes. A white couple fucks creatively on television on screens placed thoughtfully over our heads. Unlike in Bloomberg's New York, here the liberated republic allows you to smoke. Puffing hard, Ziyad looks at me.

"Why are you making this film?" he says. His twenty-two-year-old eyes are honest.

"Oh," I say, this not being the first time I have been asked this, "so that there don't have to be more people like you."

"Have you ever been to Cairo? Do you know what it means to be there, in prison, imprisoned by those who believe in the hatred of a religion that is not even yours?" says Ayad, the older of the two. He, unlike Ziyad, is a Copt, the troubled Christian minority in Egypt. He seems to have taken an instant dislike to me.

"We were not in jail for Islam," says Ziyad. "Islam had nothing to do with it. Do you think Taha Embaby was doing this for Islam?"

"Oh really? And what does the Quran say about people like you and me? Do you think that those assholes who put those lighters under your balls and their instruments in your ass were not trying to please the Islamists?"

I look at them as they lapse into Arabic. I don't understand a word. Ziyad has been here for six months, pretty much homeless, a refugee in this cold, unfeeling country. I never did like the French very much—they seem to be so self-important, and they carry the weight of their history rather heavily. I can only imagine what it is like for Ziyad here. He barely speaks the language, and the overwhelming bureaucracy of the French system around his asylum case and indeed his entire life cannot be helping. Ayad is different. He was freed from prison earlier and got asylum sooner. He can speak French and he is street smart. He gets by just fine. Our discussion shifts to the Quran, Surah 27 in the book. Fahishah (adultery, to some). Lut (Lot). I feel transplanted outside my

*Gay Travels in the Muslim World*
© 2007 by The Haworth Press, Inc. All rights reserved.
doi:10.1300/5481_11

body looking at this conversation. Here I am in Paris, talking about the Quran with two of the survivors of the Queen Boat trial. They are the lucky ones, though. They got away.

New Delhi, June 2003

"Can you please stop bothering me?"

I play the message for the fifth time on my father's answering machine. And just in the middle, the power goes off again. It's a hot summer in Delhi and I am visiting home for the first time in three years. Sadia, who has left me the message, is a twenty-three-year-old lesbian who lives in the old part of the city—the Walled City—one of the few remaining parts of Delhi that is still majority Muslim. Just a week ago, I filmed her at the Jama Masjid, one of the largest mosques in India. I follow her around with my newly acquired PD-150 camera as she walks the *galis* (walkway) wearing a burka, just a flash of red showing from her *salwar*. She stops sometimes and talks about her faith. She never uses the word *lesbian,* and I know that no affirmative words in Urdu exist other than *humjinsparast,* which is quite a tongue twister.

"I can't use that word," she says from under layers of black cotton. "You don't understand, Parvez. It's wrong to even use the word."

We have lunch at Karim's. Parathas dripping ghee and haleem, drowned with Thums Up. It's perfectly heavy for the forty-degree-Celsius heat. Sadia has been married and was supposed to go with her husband to Dubai, a better life. But he used to beat her, and she finally got a divorce. She lives with her parents, and in the small streets of Purani Dilli (Old Delhi) where there are no secrets. The only way to hide the shame of her divorce when she steps outside is the burka. She is so beautiful, frail, and young.

Educated with a masters in Islamic law, she has had an online relationship with a Pakistani lesbian in Islamabad for two years now.

"You should go to Bint el Nas. That's where I met Shazia," she tells me.

Shazia is to be married in a few months. Sadia wants to help her to freedom. But freedom where? Surely not in the crowded streets of old Delhi. And this is the same woman who will do her *namaz* prayers five times a day and be on her knees praying even more, after every time she is on the Bint el Nas Web site.

I meet her every day. We talk. We connect. A few days later she tells me that she cannot be in the film and that on judgment day she will not be able to face Allah and tell him why she did it. She wants to back out and have me give her all the footage. We start a cycle of argument and discussion. She finally says that doing the Salat al Istikhara, a prayer for Allah's guidance, will help her decide. She does it. The answer from Allah is *no* she tells me. I tell her that I can wait. A few days pass and then I call her again, begging her to meet at least as friends, no camera.

Then this message on my answering machine. "Can you please stop bothering me?" I have not heard from Sadia since.

The title of this article includes "Manufacturing Dissent" and "Work In Progress." Cryptic, but hopefully meaningful by the time I finish writing. It's a rainy early fall afternoon in Chelsea as I write this in hurried fashion. These are initial thoughts on a hesitant, evolving (for two years now), and probably problematic (to at least some of you) thesis. Let's begin with who I am and why I can even pretend to write in this anthology. I find some dissonance in being transplanted from a small town called Saharanpur in northern India, where I grew up, to New York, and writing this. As is the nature of many transplants into the American Dream, I find myself "dissonated" enough, often enough, to question my own contradictions and even my own hypocrisy. I find myself nervous about putting to paper thoughts that have engaged me a great deal in the four years and twelve days since I landed on the shores of the "free world" in my rickety boat.

So I find myself at the Big Cup in Chelsea, somewhat of a mecca for the youthful and the not-so-youthful male homosexuals within our community. I must make a confession: the Big Cup, until it closed, was a favorite *adda,* or hangout, for me. I love being a gay man, and here I found cheap coffee, free wireless access, and cute gay boys in all shapes and sizes—and one predominant color. I have in the past called the predominance of this color, in what is sometimes simplistically referred to as "Western gay male subculture," "The Unbearable Whiteness of Being." It's interesting as well, because I love my magical, mystical White Boys. And, damn it, I have not one, but *two* white boyfriends! It could probably be referenced as just my being interested in whites, or, as some more academically inclined friends have hypothesized, it could be the attraction of the colonized soul to the colonizer: getting sweet revenge through some old fashioned, action-filled buggery. Of course, as I wrote this, the reality of being in America was all too obvious; even my ever-vigilant spell-check advised me that *colour* was spelled as c-o-l-o-r and not c-o-l-o-*u*-r. So, putting on my headphones with some sweet, Hindi, Bollywood music, and trying not to be distracted by the luscious and tempting landscape of eager young eyes staring at *HX, Next, Manhunt,* and me, I sit down to write.

After I started to reimagine my life on the INS—now rechristened USCIS, or United States Citizenship and Immigration Service—calendar, I realized that today, the tenth of September, 2004 (the date

I write this) is just thirty-one days before I become illegal in the "land of the free." There is some irony to this as I begin the next phase of production of an ambitious documentary called *In the Name of Allah* with some really big names. My fate in this country is in the hands of a probably underpaid and bored clerk at the Immigration Offices in Vermont. The visa category I applied for is called "Alien with Extraordinary Ability." A friend asked what that meant, to which I flippantly replied that it meant I gave the best blow jobs on the East Coast. And, although that may well be true—and believe me there is only one way to find out—the category is a problematic one, as are the others I have found myself boxed in, often willingly and sometimes with tacit approval. These include "brown," "Muslim," "progressive Muslim," "filmmaker," "queer activist," "person of color," etc.

I was recently described to a panel I was invited to speak on as someone whose work "addresses a critical force field which, in the wake of September 11th (and as we approach another anniversary) seemed hard to imagine for many U.S. commentators: Muslim sexual diversity, community, voice, and rights. The film also raises a number of thorny questions about political representation and commercial support." This is a flattering description, and one that would be easy to agree with. I do find, however, that I am one of many well-intentioned individuals trying his or her best to work within this critical force field. However, now, two years into making a film addressing complex issues, I find myself questioning my own contradictions as a filmmaker, as someone who is trying to flourish in the most capitalist society in the world, and as a Muslim. I travel fast and I travel furious through many Islams, many different from what my childhood taught me, many about hate.

As a filmmaker I grapple with the politics of the camera—an extremely intrusive and hardly invisible instrument—as it goes into the lives of queer Muslims, lives that have, for the most part, gone unsung. As coming from what many here in the West very problematically and inaccurately call the "third world," I also find myself dealing with issues of using money kindly provided by the big names I referred to before, more specifically, the UK's Channel 4, Germany's ZDF, and Franco-German ARTE, to intrude into the lives of these communities that have been surrounded by walls of silence for way too long. And, as a Muslim, my credentials have been questioned more than once by fellow Muslim queers, coming as I do from a mixed—easily labeled "secular" in India—family. Making this film now, I am still learning what it means to be a Muslim, specifically a gay/queer Muslim, and am engaged in a rather difficult, often unproductive dialogue with an extremely unforgiving Allah.

The journey of realizing *In the Name of Allah* continues to be a long one. In fact, it has been a work in progress for so long, that friends often call me just that—a work-in-progress—these days. What started as my little graduate thesis, filmed on borrowed cameras and no money, has morphed into a huge animal that is supposed to generate good ratings for my European broadcasters, sizeable percentages for my many partners, and fame, fortune, and *fatwas* for me. The most interesting show of interest in the film I have received recently is from the much-maligned-by-mullahs MTV. I have just finished editing a trailer for them and find tremendous irony in the possibility of part of this film being financed by the "big evil one."

If Islam is indeed the fastest growing religion in the world, and if 22 percent of the world's population is indeed Muslim, it will take only a little math—with the help of Mr. Kinsey—to determine the fabulously diverse numbers of faggots, dykes, and all those in between that we are dealing with in the Muslim world. And that of course underlines another issue that this film grapples with: Islam is not the problematic monolith that the West now finds itself grappling with, but a collection of very diverse opinions, thoughts, and processes that speak in as many voices as there are groups and faiths within Islam. Making this film in this deeply divided country where the fault lines of prejudice run deeper than ever, and from within Islam, where similar fault lines erode the basic tolerance of the faith, is an interesting exercise. The politics I live in, determine every aspect of this film as well. At the risk of fast and easy deportation, I want to say the following:

*George Bush, as the unelected President of the United States of America, you have much in common with the mullahs that preach intolerance from their bully pulpits, during their Friday* khutbas, *or sermons.*

*Like them, nobody really elected you.*

*Like them, you feel that preaching the politics of hatred and intolerance for the other and for queers is your birthright.*

*Your crusade is no different from their jihad, which, by the way, in its purest, Quranic form can mean a personal journey of self-discovery and awareness, rather than a holy war.*

*You misuse your God—I've heard it's Jesus—and invoke his name wrongfully, just as they do with their Allah.*

And this is where the documentary we are trying to make comes in. *In the Name of Allah* has always been a truly independent film, and if independent filmmaking is like guerilla warfare, then this film comes to you from the trenches. As it emerges, built with the contradictions of the so-called East and the so-called West, the contradictions of its filmmaker, and, indeed, the contradictions of the faith it tries to defend, it deals with the contradictions of creating faith, tolerance, and understanding in a filmmaking world, where the exchange of dollars and euros is fundamental to the process itself.

It's hard to describe to a commissioning editor sitting somewhere in Paris, Berlin, London, or New York the lives put at stake by the very act of appearing in this film. Other than the heat and dust, the power failures, taps that run dry, and phones that die, the reality of existence in Delhi, Cairo, Karachi, or Kabul is a very different one. Sitting at the Big Cup in Chelsea, the contrast cannot be greater. A photographer from *HX* magazine is eagerly taking pictures of six semipubescent gay boys dressed in their Gap Ts and very gelled hair. We are informed that this is for the "Back to School" issue of the magazine and, to reflect the true diversity of America, and indeed American homosexuals, the group includes four white boys; one brown, Latino-looking boy; and one Asian, probably Chinese, boy. Surely this is the manufacture of the new gay image in process. Can we easily underestimate the reach of *HX*? And what about shows like *The L-Word, Boy Meets Boy, Will & Grace,* and *Queer As Folk,* which I have on more than one occasion referred to as "White as Fuck"? Where does that really leave the poor gay or lesbian Muslim? Oppressed, of course, by many Muslims. And not even included, of course, in most "gay subculture" discourse.

As we try and construct the first real and comprehensive image of these unlikely creatures—to be PC: the gay, lesbian, bisexual, transgendered, and queer Muslims—we must realize that these terms are a Western construct. Let me be clear: none of these categories means anything to many of my friends living in Cairo or Islamabad. If anything, the languages they speak—Farsi, Arabic, Urdu, Punjabi, and Bengali—have very few words of affirmation to describe the "odd" and "unnatural" behaviors, so to speak, that we indulge in. The cinematic representation of these complex identities therefore comes with many of the challenges of almost developing a new language.

And then there are the contradictions of Islam itself. In the early years of the Abbasid empire, in a region that would include present-day Baghdad, the Arab poet Abu Nuwas, a favorite of the Caliphs, flourished. Nuwas wrote a kind of verse that would not easily be accepted in a moralistic society like America. Let's sample some. And I quote in J.W. Wright's translation:

> Oh Sulayman, sing to me and give me a cup of wine
> And if the wine comes round, seize it and give it to me!
> Give me a cup of distraction from the Muezzin's call
> Give me wine to drink publicly
> And bugger and fuck me now!

Abu Nuwas, whose risqué verse did get the better of him eventually, went on to take *ayahs*—or verses—17 and 22 from *surah*—or chapter—56 of the Quran and transform it into a homoerotic fantasy, filled with "beautiful lads" with "fingers dyed with henna" serving wine. What many of us don't know is that all Muslims, like the eager, young, intifada-angst-filled Palestinians who blow themselves up, are promised not just seventy virgins bearing wine, but also young boys serving the same forbidden liquid in paradise. Abu Nuwas's grave is somewhere in suburban Baghdad and has no doubt been reduced to rubble by the eager bombs dispatched by teen marines.

In the construction of the image and life of the "queer" Muslim is also the awareness of the not so well-known fact that a sexual revolution of immense proportions came to the earliest Muslims, some 1,300 years before the West had even thought it. This promise of equal gender rights and, unlike in the Bible, the stress on sex within the confines of marriage as not just for reproduction but also for enjoyment has all but been lost in the rhetoric spewing from loudspeakers perched on *masjids,* or mosques, in Riyadh, Marrakech, and Islamabad. The same Islam that has for centuries not only tolerated but also openly celebrated homosexuality is, today, used to justify a state-sanctioned pogrom against gay men in Egypt—America's "enlightened" friend in the Middle East.

I have spent considerable time filming with Ziyad. After almost two years in an Egyptian prison he was recently granted asylum in France. Unfortunately, the French system gave him nothing beyond that, and treated him with contempt. He now lives a penniless life on the streets of Paris, trying desperately to learn the language of his new country. He can never go back to Egypt. Describing his time in custody to me and also to my friend Scott Long, who compiled a report on the Egypt situation for Human Rights Watch, this is what Ziyad had to say about some of his adventures in custody:

"I go inside. Heaven help us, this guy is sitting in a chair. I had a position before I was arrested, in the family, in the neighborhood. The biggest bully would call me Mr. Ziyad. And this man spoke me to me like a child . . .

"Then the head man, Fakhry Saleh, walks in. 'Strip, kneel.' Oh, he talked to me like a dog. I got down on all fours. I had taken my pants off. I assumed the position. He said, 'No, no, this will not do. Get your chest down and your ass up.'

"I said 'I can't' and I started crying hysterically. And he said, 'All these things you are doing will not cut any ice with me. Be quick about it; we've got work to do.' I still could not control myself at all. He said, 'Shut up, everything is clear and we can see it in front of us.' First, he looked and felt me up. Suddenly six doctors came in. What is there about my anus? They all felt me up, each in turn, pulling my buttocks apart.

"They brought this feather against my anus and tickled it. Apparently that was not enough. So they brought out the heavy artillery. After the feather came the fingers. Then they stuck something else inside. I would cry and he would stick stuff inside and I would cry and he would stick more.

"I hoped that they would feel sorry from all the crying, but they didn't, they did not seem to feel anything. Fakhry said after, 'Why didn't you cry when men put their things in you?' I wanted to spit on him. But I was still crying."

Chillingly, Ziyad repeats the same story to me that he told Scott many months earlier in Cairo. This has to be true.

How can the documentary filmmaker therefore exploit this story for mass consumption? Surely, the desire to bring it out is a noble one, but the exchange of money as a necessity for filmmaking without Ziyad benefiting from it financially, penniless as he is, presents a conundrum. The producer of *In the Name of Allah* is Sandi DuBowski, a Jewish filmmaker who achieved tremendous success, both financial and artistic, with his film *Trembling Before G-d.* Sandi and I see a tremendous similarity in our journeys and our faiths. Working together we hope that, as gay filmmakers, we can open a necessary dialogue between Islam and Judaism, both religions—along with Christianity—born from the same father, in the same, now contested desert. However, it is interesting to note that more than one character I have filmed with in the past two years has dropped out of the film, not wanting yet another dialogue on Islam to have Jewish or American complicity in it. But where has the media or the cinema of the West truly allowed Muslims to wield power and money?

My friend Jim De Seve, who has just made a remarkable documentary on gay marriage called *Tying The Knot,* is at the forefront of that debate today in this hot, American summer of politics in which the issue is suddenly one of national importance. Often it seems of more national importance than the shameful sexual and physical abuse of prisoners at Abu Ghraib, which more than one commissioning editor has encouraged me to document. As Jim travels this landscape and becomes a filmmaker and, foremost, an activist, I wonder how many years will it take for my Muslim brothers and sisters to engage in a similar discussion. Is it even a necessary debate? After all, "gay" men, or, more accurately, men who enjoyed sex with men, were marrying one another in the Egyptian oasis of Siwa just fifty years ago.

Michael Luongo, who is bringing this anthology to life, is constantly engaged in the admirable task of writing about gay travels in the Muslim world, including in Kabul. It might be easy to dismiss him, saying that here is yet another white man creating the next frontier for gay tourism, and we might wonder how long it will be before planeloads of Chelsea boys descend upon the locals in Kabul. But I see Michael engaged in a task far more important. Writing in the gay mainstream press, he is actually creating the first, post-Taliban, nonacademic media representation of Muslim men who have celebrated their love for one another openly and for centuries.

The personal is the political, and in making *In the Name of Allah* I must face up to my own political beliefs. The precarious torch that the lady on the Hudson holds has never burnt more feebly.

Manufacturing consent is all that the powers in Islam and in the West have successfully done. And, unfortunately, the liberal left that so many queer Western ideologies are naturally attracted to has done little to counter it. In closing thoughts, I need to stress a different kind of manufacture: that of dissent. Let's make a deal. While you all try and do it here in the United States in a more productive fashion, I shall try and do it in the Muslim "worlds." I shall go with my camera and some of my anger and take this film and this dialogue to the mullahs and the *masjids* where they hide. But there is more to the bargain. I hope for a change that can be more constructive. To a conservative Christian family sitting in rural Alabama, the crusaders for gay marriage, abortion rights, and peace, with their ragged T-shirts with angry, clever slogans, must evoke a reaction that might go like this: *See, I told you so. Look at them. What about family? And do they even have a job?*

Let us imagine a new kind of crusade. The cool, air-conditioned corridors of Western Academia, lined with books and ideas, are just not enough. Don't get me wrong: ideas are good and vital. Hell, ideas are just what make us human. But it's time to get our hands dirty, my dear readers. *In the Name of Allah* is the beginning of a crusade.

Allow me to use another example to better illustrate my point. Arundhati Roy, the mistress of words and ideas, as she stands on a pedestal at Riverside Church exhorts the so-called American Left to change. She is sari clad, mysterious, and dark with kohl-lined eyes. She is smart and she is sexy. She tells her throngs of well-meaning admirers that what Mr. Bush and his gang of war criminals export to Iraq and Afghanistan is "Instant Mix Imperial Democracy—Bring to Boil, Add Oil, and then Bomb." It's heady to listen to the intoxicating, catchy language of ideas coming from the luscious lips of a frail woman coming from a country far, far away and then go back to the East Village, to *Democracy Now!,* or to any of the idea-rich hangouts of this battle-scarred city I live in. But it's hard to do what Ms. Roy did so successfully. A Delhi socialite with a genius-like ability to write, she transformed herself into a tireless, often controversial, and much reviled-in-India crusader. She went out and used the power of her privileged education and her words—and her appearance—to make her voice heard and to even force thought. She got her hands dirty.

I know I am preaching perhaps to the choir here. When are we going to stop talking to ourselves? When will we own up the privilege of living in the world's most "developed" country? There needs to be an understanding of the privilege that comes even to the poor in America. And there needs to be change. If this is the world's most capitalistic society, it does understand the language of a consumer economy. Dissent has been manufactured too long among ourselves, on the assembly lines of our self-indulgent ideas. Let's take it now to those who oppose us and talk in a language they can understand. Let's manufacture dissent, and consume ideas, knowledge, and tolerance. Let's decide here that together this will be our Project for a Newer American Century.

Let's together—travel gay—through the richness of Islam. Let's get our hands dirty and let's please manufacture dissent.

## ॐ 12                 Paradox

*Thomas Bradbury*

"I can't get on my flight," I said into the cell phone.

"Why not?" Askin said.

"I made a big mistake. I booked the flight but I never got the tickets and the airline cancelled my reservations and now the flight is sold out."

I was nervous, thinking he was about to read me the riot act, but instead he just said, "Oh."

This was a particularly humiliating situation for me because I am a travel agent. I am like the cobbler's son who has no shoes. How could I have made such a stupid mistake? Now, I had to think. How was I going to get to Askin? I had only three days for this trip, and I needed to see him.

Askin and I had been apart for almost four months, and I longed to see him. The airport in Istanbul was packed with people stranded, and many of them were at the standby counter with me trying to get on fully booked flights.

"Listen, I think I can get on a flight to Antalya and I will rent a car and drive down." He hesitated. He rarely told me not to do anything, but I waited.

"Okay, be care," he said, making a grammatical error.

I wasn't particularly thrilled with the idea of having to drive three-and-a-half hours at night, but I really didn't want to wait. The flight the next morning was sold out as well. I was about to do something I told my clients never to do—drive at night in Turkey.

I called my business partner Seren and told her what I was doing. Could she get me a car in Antalya that I would drop off in Dalaman on Sunday? She called back. All the car companies in Antalya were

*Gay Travels in the Muslim World*
Published by The Haworth Press, Inc., 2007. All rights reserved.
doi:10.1300/5481_12

sold out except Hertz, and they wanted 100 million lira a day and a 95 euro drop fee. It was going to cost me as much to get to him as it had cost me to fly from New York to Istanbul. What should I do? It was too much. Maybe I should just spend the night in Antalya and take the bus down the next day.

Seren reasoned with me, "You don't want to do that. Listen, just take the car and go."

"Okay, but listen I think there is a shortcut down. Can you call Hasan (our local agent in Kas) and ask him for directions on that road and call me back?" She said she would do it and get back to me.

Upon arrival in Antalya, with a new Ford Fiesta from Hertz and directions from Hasan, I began my drive, through the mountains, in Turkey, at night. This is a particularly dangerous because Turkey is notorious for having trucks, tractors, scooters, and even horse-drawn wagons on their highways at night without lights. You think you are on a road by yourself doing 120 kilometers an hour and suddenly come upon an apparition doing 20. I took a deep breath, told myself to stay alert and got going.

Two hours later, my cell phone rang. "Where are you?"

"I am outside Demre."

"One and a half hours later, you are here."

"Okay, I will call you when I am closer."

An hour later my cell phone rings again. This time more urgently, he asks, "Where are you?"

"I am in Fethiye."

"Half hour later now."

Sometime later another call, this time angrily, "Where are you?"

"Askin, I am almost there."

"Ha," he says, hanging up on me.

Arriving at his house, I am concentrating on parking as he suddenly appears beside the car. He startles me at first, but then I see the big smile on his face. He had grown a mustache and goatee since the last time I saw him. I wondered where he'd gotten the idea for this new, modern, Western style, but it suited him. He shook my hand and kissed me on both cheeks, the traditional Turkish greeting. This for the benefit of watching neighbors. And they were always watching.

Askin and I had met ten years earlier on my first trip to Turkey. I had booked into a small hotel on the Mediterranean. It was late when I arrived and I asked at the desk if I could still eat something. The clerk said that I could, and he led me to the hotel's restaurant. I was the only one there, and Askin became my waiter. After my meal he asked if I wanted to finish my wine in the bar.

The bar was done in Anatolian style, with cushions on the floor and the walls covered in Turkish carpets and fabrics. He sat down next to me and started to talk to me. His English was limited, my Turkish nonexistent. Out of nowhere he suddenly leaned over and kissed me. He said, "Go to your room. I will be there in an hour." It was two days before Christmas, and I felt like I'd just been given a very special gift. I spent five days in that hotel—three days longer than I'd expected. Every chance he got he'd visit me in my room. It was my best Christmas ever.

When I returned to New York I looked back on our time together as simply a vacation fling, but one day I had a sudden urge to call him. When I called the hotel, he was the one who answered.

"I have not been happy since you left," he told me.

I immediately made plans to go back and see him in a month. He told me it would not be good for him to meet me there and that we should meet in a larger city. He said if his brothers found out about us they would kill him.

So began a pattern. We would always meet away from his hometown. On some occasions there were things that would happen that would leave me wondering, but I would always assume they had to do with our cultural differences. Our first fight happened when we were sitting talking with a group of boys at a small pension in Antalya. Askin said something that I knew was patently untrue, and as I was just learning Turkish, I jokingly said *"yalancı"* (liar) to him. He got up immediately from the table and went storming off to our room. When I would call him at home I would hear children in the background. When I asked about it, he simply explained that he lived with his sister and her children. Her husband was off working in Hopa on the Georgian border.

I was excited the first time we were going to Istanbul together. In a cosmopolitan city like that I thought we could be more comfortable and he would be more open. As a surprise, I decided to take him to a very nice gay bar I knew there. It was on the top floor of a building, with a beautiful 360-degree view of the Bosphorus. Askin took one look around and fled. I chased after him, asking what was the matter, but he just kept walking. When we got back to our hotel room he turned and looked at me and said, "I am not gay."

I was incredulous. "What are you talking about?" We had been in bed together not more than a few hours earlier.

"I am not gay," he replied. "I like gay people, I like to look at gay people, but I am not gay." I was completely befuddled, but didn't know what to say in response to him. On our next trip to Istanbul he asked me to take him to a gay bar.

On another trip to Antalya, a Dutch woman friend who was married to a Turk told me, "Look, this is a village man. His family is going to expect him to get married. He will have to marry someday. It isn't so much that he is with you but his family will force him to marry. To not marry in a village is just not done." I remembered how once we had met a friend of his in a restaurant. His friend asked if I was married, and when I said no he appeared visibly shocked. Later when I asked Askin why his friend had reacted like that he answered with typical Turkish bluntness, "Because you are old." (I was forty.)

Later that night, when we were in bed together, I asked him, "Is this true what Emmy told me? Will you have to marry someday?" He answered that yes, he would.

"The day you get married is the last day we are together," I told him.

He was very moody for a long time after that, but then one day, suddenly, everything changed. I asked him what had caused the improvement. He told me it was because he had decided not to marry. I was happy.

After a couple of years of long-distance commuting I decided to take a leave of absence from my job to spend six months in Turkey. I wanted to know if we could make a go of it together. We had been unsuccessful in getting him an American visa, so I thought I would just move there. When I told him my plan he was less than enthusiastic, but he wouldn't tell me not to come. He was between jobs, and I said we could travel in Turkey together and see if we could find someplace to live in his country, someplace where we could both be comfortable together.

When I got there, he met me in Antalya and we spent a week together. He said he had to go home to take care of some business and he would meet me in Bodrum in a week. Yet, when I got there, he didn't show up. I started calling his house.

The woman who answered the phone said he was working and she couldn't reach him either. I was worried, but I also knew that this was Turkey and this is the kind of thing that happened here. When I finally reached him he said he had to take a job and they didn't have a phone where he was working but he would try to join me in Bozcaada in a week. When I got to Bozcaada he said he couldn't come. In the meantime, another Turkish friend had joined me on my travels, and since we were having quite a good time traveling together I decided to ignore my problems with Askin for the time being.

Askin continued to put me off. I decided to go to his village and find out for myself what was going on. I was furious with him. I didn't approach him directly because I didn't want to put him in harm's way, but I did want to talk to him and find out what was going on. I thought maybe our affair had run its course. It wouldn't have been the first time. I was so frustrated and confused by everything that had happened that I finally confessed my affair to a young American woman working in the hotel where I was staying. She had lived in Turkey far longer than I had. Affairs between foreigners and Turks are nothing out of the ordinary, and I thought she might be able to decipher the mysteries of my relationship. A couple of days later she said, "I have to tell you something that Tom from the travel agency said to me the other day. He said, 'You should see Askin's two sons. They are the most adorable children I have ever seen.'"

I said, "Oh no, those aren't his children, they're his nephews, his sister's children."

"I don't think so," she answered.

I decided to get to the bottom of this. I knew one of the other men who worked in the hotel was related to him, and the next morning I screwed up the courage and asked him in Turkish, "Do you remember Askin who used to work here? Is he married?"

He said, "Oh yes, he is my *Abi*. [literally older brother, but in this case his older cousin]. He has two boys."

I was sick at heart. I went downstairs and called my friend Emmy. "Askin is married. I am leaving and never seeing him again. It's over."

Emmy counseled, "Of course it's over. It has to be, but I know that he loves you and you must go and talk to him."

The next morning I went to where he was working. I knew he would be alone. We went in the back and sat down.

I blurted out, "I know you are married!"

He burst into tears. "Who told you?"

"Why didn't *you* tell me?" I demanded.

"You said if I was married we were finished." I remembered my ultimatum. He said, "Please come back at noon and I will take you to meet my family."

I decided I had nothing to lose. It was over and I might as well meet them. I was curious.

As we were driving to his house he told me he had married when he was very young, only seventeen. His wife was from his small village, and it had been an arranged marriage. She was a very good woman and he loved her like a sister. When I arrived at their house I gave his wife a present I had brought, some Turkish pottery. In the traditional Turkish way she put it to one side and didn't open it in front of me. The boys were truly adorable, and they were all over Askin, kissing and hugging him. The littlest one, five at the time, hung on him. They brought out photo albums of the family and showed me pictures of the older one's *sunnet,* the traditional Muslim circumcision. I was a little shocked that they even had pictures of the boy's penis after the operation. Surprising in a country of great modesty.

After having tea, Askin said we should drive to his family vineyard and meet his father and mother, a half hour away. His father had lived in Germany for many years as a pharmacist and was very frustrated that as a foreigner I could not speak German. Askin barbecued some meat and we ate on the floor in the typical Anatolian way.

As we were leaving his father said to me, "Don't forget us."

Over the years, I had resolved many times to break it off with Askin. Once I went so far as to say to him, "Listen, this isn't working. Let's stop."

He answered, "No we have been together this long. I am not breaking up with you!"

We have been together for almost ten years now. It has been said that I am a commuter to Turkey. I am not sure why the relationship has lasted. The cultural differences, and that it is a long-distance relationship may keep it going. It hasn't been smooth sailing, and there are many times when it feels too hard, but then there are moments of intense satisfaction.

So now I am back, and he is taking the luggage into the house. At the door his wife, Anet, is waiting for me.

"*Hos geldin, Abi,*" she greets me warmly. (Welcome older brother.)

"*Hos bulduk,* Anet," I reply. (It is good to see you.)

As I sit down on the couch, the youngest one comes running out of his bedroom, eyes just barely open, sleep all over his face.

"*Amca,*" he whispers. (Uncle.) He climbs up into my lap and wraps his arms tightly around my neck.

I feel content. Reunited with my lover, holding his child in my arms. Anet enters with the tea. I am home.

# ❧ 13 The Galilee

*David C. Muller*

At the age of eighteen I became a full time soldier. I was given an M16 and told to guard a base near Binyamina. At first I thought this job was really important, to be guarding this base, but then I figured out the base was nothing more than a giant storage facility. After that, I spent long hours wandering along the perimeter fence thinking about the moment I'd be able to leave and go home to my family in the north of Israel.

Back then, I came from a moshav called Metzitzah, a really small collective town, kind of like a kibbutz, but without all the socialist mediocrity. As a kid I hated living there because everybody knew everyone else's business, but after a few months of basic training in the army, I was always thrilled to get back to my family whenever I could. Rarely did my commander let me leave the base, but when he did, I fled like my life depended on it.

I almost always took a taxi on my way home, a shared taxi. We call it a *monit sherut* in Hebrew. It's really just a van people hop on and off of as it drives from town to town. I usually caught one of these taxis just west of Haifa to hitch a ride inland on the road headed toward Dirhana, the closest town to my moshav. Dirhana is an Arab village. The northern part of Israel is home to many Arabs, and Dirhana is a town populated by what we called "friendly Arabs" who, for the most part, keep to themselves and refrain from acts of agitation against the Jewish State. That, however, doesn't mean the Arab residents of Dirhana, or any other Arab village for that matter, are not subjected to suspicion and dirty looks from their Jewish Israeli neighbors. But one time, right here in the Jewish State of Israel, the tables turned on me.

I was on my way home when I climbed up into a taxi, clad in my Israeli army fatigues, carrying my duffle bag with my M16 hanging off my shoulder. As I took my seat I realized I was the only Jew in a taxi filled with Arab passengers; even the driver was Arab. All the other passengers, in addition to being Arabs, were also civilians. They each turned to look at me in their own special, suspicious way, glancing down at my gun repeatedly in resentful fear. In some way, I felt what it was like to be looked at suspiciously, but, either way, I just slipped on my sunglasses and stared out the window at the passing scenery.

So there I was, sitting in this taxi, minding my own business, when I heard this obnoxious electric music decimate the otherwise silent ride. I turned my head and noticed a skinny Arab kid sitting across the aisle from me. He was devastatingly slender and dressed in a black tank top and tight red capri pants. Through my dark sunglasses I eyed this skinny Arab kid and watched him answer his cell phone. I could tell he was cute, even though his hair was crisp with styling gel and his face was hidden by knockoff designer sunglasses. I looked him up and down as I strained my ear to eavesdrop on his wireless conversation. In Arabic-accented Hebrew he told whomever he was speaking to that he was on his way and that he'd be there shortly. He said words like *yallah* and *sabahba,* soon and okay, before he said the English "bye-bye" and closed the phone.

I remember two things after that: one, that he was wearing open-toed sandals, and two, that I lowered my sunglasses so I could look at his open-toed sandals. I remember he had cute little toes and, for some reason, that made me smile. I let my eyes wander over his thin, youthful physique as he sat effortlessly across from me, and I remember cocking my head to the side trying to determine his age. Was he seventeen, eighteen, nineteen? I asked myself, *How cute do I think he is?* My jaw fell agape as I sat there and stared at him in wonder.

And then I saw this kid turn his head suddenly to look at me over his knockoff sunglasses. He looked me right in the eye, catching me staring at him. I scrambled for a second as I pushed my sunglasses up the bridge of my nose, quickly turning my attention back to the window, focusing my gaze once again on the passing scenery. I'll admit it, I was kind of embarrassed that he caught me, and I was relieved when the taxi stopped at the junction for the road that leads up to my moshav.

I hurriedly tossed my duffle bag over my shoulder and stumbled out of the taxi. Somehow the straps of my bag got tangled together with the straps of my M16 and I had to drop everything on the ground to stop for a readjustment before I could continue. I didn't look up as the taxi pulled away from the curb, but once all the straps were in order, I picked up my bag and my gun and started walking toward a road sign that said "Metzitzah" in Hebrew, Arabic, and English.

Much to my surprise, I noticed that the skinny Arab kid had also stepped down from the taxi, and as I started up the road to my moshav I saw him walking about two yards ahead of me, heading up the exact same road.

Again, I stared at him, this time my line of vision fell on his backside. The boy was very thin and tall, especially for an Arab. He had a nice butt, round and fit and framed nicely by the red capris. As I watched him walking ahead of me I noticed a strut; it looked like he was walking with a swish in his step. I smirked for a second and kind of giggled as my eyes scanned up and down the kid's body. Just as my eyes came to a pause on his ankles, he stopped moving and flipped around suddenly.

"I saw you looking at me in the *sherut,*" he said, and he took off his sunglasses. "Are you following me?" This skinny Arab kid spoke to me in Hebrew and stared at me for a longer-than-necessary moment. "Well?"

I too stopped walking. I opened my lips and said, "I'm not following you."

"Well then," he slipped the sunglasses over his eyes, "what *are* you doing?"

I squinted my eyes through my sunglasses. Something about him struck me as different. His tone, as I remember it, was not haughty or hostile. He wasn't speaking with a thorny, accusatory irritation. No, his tone was decidedly flirtatious. I watched him for a second as he pulled a small belt bag around his body.

*"Nu?"* he said, an Isreali expression meaning *well*. He unzipped the bag and took out a cigarette, "Well, are you following me? Why are you following me?"

"I'm . . . uh . . . going home." I nudged my head toward the road. "I live up on the moshav."

"Ah," he popped out his leg as he lit the cigarette, "you live up there, do you?"

I nodded, "Yeah."

He said nothing, instead he casually took a drag from his cigarette.

It was just the two of us. We were completely alone standing out there on this road looking at each other. He stared at me and smoked his cigarette while I stupidly tried to think of something to say.

I asked him, "Do you live around here?" It was the best I could come up with.

The skinny Arab boy nodded his head, "Yeah."

"Do you live in Metzitzah?"

He shook his head, "No."

"Mmm," I nodded my head slowly, never once taking my eyes off him. I smiled slightly and said, "So you, uh, got a name?"

"Yeah."

"What do people call you?"

"Busie."

"Busie?" I asked him, "You mean short for Bustan?"

"Uh-huh." He took a drag off his cigarette, "What are you called?"

I smiled. "Dudu."

"Dudu?" The Arab boy smiled for the first time. "That's cute."

I laughed under my breath and started walking along the road, "So, you're from Dirhana. Aren't you a little far from home?"

The Arab boy started walking beside me. "I never said I'm from Dirhana."

"Oh?" I asked him, "Where do you live? In Tzalmon or some place?"

"Yes," he nudged his head to the left, "over that way."

"What are you doing here? Why did you get off at this place?"

"I got off here for the same reason you were looking at me on the *sherut*."

I didn't know what to say. I thought maybe there'd been some sort of misunderstanding, but his Hebrew was clearly fluent. I dropped my eyes to the gravel of the road and saw his open-toed sandals again.

"How old are you?" he asked me. "Eighteen?"

"Yeah," turning to look at him, I noticed his profile and thought for a moment that he could pass for a Yemenite Jew; he did not necessarily look like an Arab. "How old are you?"

He smiled and nodded his head curtly, "I'm old enough."

"Old enough for what?"

He leaned his head toward me, allowing me to see his eyes behind the sunglasses, "What do you think?" He looked back up at the road and asked, "You got a place up in Metzitzah?"

Now, I must say, I'm no idiot or novice; I knew where this was headed. I knew what this skinny Arab kid wanted from me, the newly deployed Israeli soldier. But we were about twenty minutes away from my family's house on the moshav so I decided to tap dance around the big issue I knew he wanted desperately to discuss.

Instead of answering his question directly, I answered him by asking questions of my own. "What do you mean, do I have a place?" "Do *you* have family in Metzitzah?" "Where exactly do you come from?" "How old are you? Don't you ever eat?"

His answers were vague and noncommittal. He dodged my questions by talking without saying anything, answering, "I've never been to Metzitzah" and "I walk a lot."

After about five or six minutes of this, I felt like he was giving me the run around, but I let any worry I might've had dissipate. This skinny Arab kid was just . . . well . . . skinny. So skinny that if he tried anything with me I knew I could've easily broken him in half like a twig and, had I been unable to do that, I was armed with an M16. I didn't think he was going to start anything dangerous for me. If he was starting anything, I was pretty sure he wanted it to end up in the bedroom.

We walked quickly and arrived at the gate to the moshav. The Arab boy stopped for a moment to drop his second cigarette on the ground. I watched as he set the toe of his brown sandal on the cigarette butt, turning his leg slowly from side to side, like a choreographed dancer.

"So," I took off my sunglasses as the wind blew through my hair, "you want a drink or something?"

He said, "I want to see where you live."

For a second, the thought that maybe, possibly, this little Arab boy might be a spy for Hamas or Hezbollah or some terrorist group entered my mind. It was not unheard of for terrorists to sneak into a moshav or a kibbutz or some place like that and attack innocent people, but there was something disarming about this kid. Still, just to be on the safe side, I asked to see his identification card and he very willingly showed it to me. Bustan, I read, came from a nearby town called Arava, and the identification card told me he was an Arab Muslim. I was tempted to ask him to leave the card with the guard at the gate, but in the end I figured if he was going to do something bad, he would've done it by now.

"You have a cell phone?" I asked him, then took out my own. "What's your number?"

He read off some digits and I dialed the number. Seconds later I heard the obnoxious electrical ring of his phone, and I saved his number. After all that, I led him through the gates of my moshav and toward my house.

As we walked, he asked me, "You're a homo, right?"

I shrugged my shoulders and said, "Yeah, but you're one, too, aren't you?"

He smiled. "I just wanted to know for sure. You could be leading me to my death. I'm an Arab and you're a Jew and this is a moshav. Something bad could happen to me."

"It's funny you should say that," I said. "I was kind of worried about the same thing. Something bad could happen to me because I'm a Jew walking into a moshav with an Arab."

"Don't worry," he told me, "I'm not like that. Besides, you're the one with the gun; if anyone should be nervous, it should be me."

The reality was many Arabs worked in or around my moshav. I suppose that's why none of the neighbors along the main road through Metzitzah bothered to look up at me coming home with my new friend. Many of the other moshavniks were accustomed to seeing Arabs of all ages coming and going in and out of our community. If my neighbors noticed anything amiss, it was that Bustan looked like a skinny little gay kid more than anything else.

My family, at the time, lived right next door to an old Jewish woman named Orlah. Orlah's husband had died a few years earlier and, shortly thereafter, she became the nosy neighbor of Metzitzah. On the day I walked past her house with Bustan striding alongside me, Orlah was standing in the middle of her tiny front yard watering her lawn. I saw her and nodded my head, but she just stared at us, her two old beady eyes glancing from me to him and back again. I imagine she quickly deduced that the boy walking with me was an Arab, and I saw her initial look of curiosity transform into a scowl. I thought about mentioning something to her in passing about whether or not she was in violation of the moshav water ration, but I said nothing as my new Arab friend and I walked past her house in silence.

At my house only my mom was home. My dad was still at work and my younger sister was still at school. Thankfully, to make a long, uninteresting saga short, my mom and dad adhere to an Israeli moshav mentality and, as a result, they have what I call a hands-off approach to parenting. With two older brothers already finished with requisite military service, my mom was not overly worried about my safety as are other moms who had kids away in the army. That's not to say she wasn't thrilled to see me. She was, and she gave me a hug when I came in, and asked about the skinny Arab kid who came in right after me.

"He's a friend of a friend," I told my mother. "He lives nearby, and his brother is in my unit but stuck back at the base on guard duty."

"Oh," my mom smiled nicely at the boy.

"I have something I . . . uh," I looked at Bustan and smirked. "I have something I want to give him."

The kid was not without manners, and he held out his hand to my mom and said, "Hi, I'm Bustan."

My mom smiled. "Nice to meet you," she even shook his hand and then added, "I have to go pick up your sister at the school and then we're going to Vatami's place in Lotem for dinner."

"Okay." I dropped my duffle bag on the floor and finally removed the gun from my shoulder.

My mom asked, "Will you be alright if I go now?"

I just waved my hands and shushed her away. "Yes, Mom, I'll be fine."

"Do you need a ride someplace?" She turned to Bustan. "I'm taking the car if you need to get somewhere."

"Mom!" I whined suddenly. "I said I'll be fine."

"I'm just asking." My Israeli mother suddenly became a Jewish mother. "But if you don't want me to worry about you, then fine!" She grabbed the keys from a bowl sitting on a side table. "I'll just leave you two here alone by yourselves."

"Fine," I started to unbutton the green shirt of my uniform. "Just go then."

My mom left immediately after that.

I took off my shirt and led Bustan up to my room. I'd grown up sharing a room with the younger of my two older brothers and, since I'd left for the army, my dad had come in and taken down all of our posters. The room was uncharacteristically devoid of any youthful personality, except for the bright blue sheets on the bed.

"Well, okay," I said, "here we are." I sat on the corner of the bed and started to unlace my boots. I watched him out of the corner of my eye. He looked around the room before he stepped out of his sandals. I remember he had nice feet, and I remember feeling my dick grow hard in my pants. I stood up and quickly readjusted myself and started to unbuckle my belt. Bustan watched my hands flutter around the waist of my uniform.

"Take your dick out," he said.

I said, "Take *your* dick out." I cut right to the chase. "Let me see *your* cock and balls."

Bustan turned off his cell phone and took off his black tank top. He unlaced the red string that held the fly of his pants together, and in one deft movement he exposed everything he had to offer. I took a good look at his penis. He was pretty well hung, but he needed a shave. His testicles, much to my surprise, were the biggest set of balls I've ever seen before or since.

Of course, it came as no surprise that we found ourselves completely naked, rolling around on top of those bright blue sheets about ten seconds later. Unfortunately for us, I didn't know how long we had before my family returned to the house, so we only gave each other head before we, surprisingly, shot our loads at exactly same time. Afterward we quietly put our clothes back on and left my house.

I walked him out to the gate of the moshav and told him, "Listen, I had a really great time. You've got some nice lips."

He smiled faintly and lit a cigarette. "Well, thank you."

"I'd like to do this again sometime, if you're willing."

He inhaled and exhaled and then giggled and smiled. "Okay," he said and nodded, "sure. But next time I want to do more than just oral."

"Yeah." Here's where I got my chance to smile. "Me too."

"You have my number."

"I do?"

"Don't you remember? You called me the last time we were right here."

"Oh yeah," I nodded. "Well, in that case, I'll definitely be calling you next time I come home."

"How often do you come home?"

"About once a month or so."

"Sounds good to me." He smoked his cigarette slowly. "What's your name again?"

"Dudu."

"That's not your real name, is it?"

I shook my head. "Only my mom calls me David."

"Hmm," the skinny Arab kid nodded disinterestedly. "Alright then, well," he said and glanced out at the road, "I have to go now."

"So I can call you?"

"Yeah." He started walking. "Call me the next time you come."

"Okay."

That was it, I watched him walk down the road a bit before I waved to the guard at the gate, the same one who'd seen us earlier, and then I started up back toward my house. A day and a half later I returned to my base near Binyamina and forgot all about this skinny Arab kid.

Thirty some odd days later I found myself on my way home from the army, clad in my Israeli fatigues with a duffle bag and the same M16 as before hanging over my shoulder. On the inland road west of Haifa, I climbed up into another shared taxi, this one again filled with Arabs; even the driver was Arab, and, as luck would have it, Bustan was sitting across from me once again. I was dressed the same, only the sunglasses were new, and he looked the same as before except now he was wearing a pair of blue jeans. Everything happened much the same way it had a month earlier.

However, this time Bustan was not talking on his cell phone. In fact, he wasn't doing much of anything except staring out the window. He did not acknowledge me; he only ignored me. Because of my uniform and the gun and because of the dirty looks the other Arab passengers were discreetly giving me, I basically ignored him also. Then my stop came up and I got down out of the shared taxi, and again, just like the last time, the straps of my bag became tangled with the straps of my gun. But this time, I noticed the skinny Arab kid before I stopped to put my bag down and readjust all those pesky straps.

I listened to the taxi pull away from the curb before I looked up at him and said, "Oh hey . . . hi. What's up?"

He popped out his leg and lit a cigarette. "You never called me."

"I was going to call you when I got home."

Bustan appeared unimpressed with my response.

"This is the first time I've been back home since the last time we . . . you know." I flashed a friendly smile.

"Really?" The Arab boy took a drag and stared at me stoically, his face partially hidden behind his dark sunglasses.

He stared at me and smoked his cigarette while I stupidly tried to think of something to say. Unlike our last encounter, this time words escaped me.

"So," he said flatly, "aren't you going to invite me up for a drink?"

"Uh . . ." hustling to untangle all my straps, I hoisted up my duffle bag and said, "Yeah, sure."

"Is your mom there?"

I shrugged my shoulders and started walking. "I don't know, but if she is, I'm sure we can come up with something."

Bustan came up next to me and we headed up the road to Met-zitzah. We barely talked as we walked but I asked him how he'd been since the last time I'd seen him. He said *sabahba* and *yofi* and things like that, but he never asked me anything. We passed the guard at the gate, a different guard this time, as we walked up the main road of the moshav. This time Orlah was gone; she wasn't standing in her front yard watering her lawn when we passed by her house.

"I wonder where that evil nosy neighbor is today." I nodded toward Orlah's conspicuously vacant-looking residence. "Usually the old bag is out here spying on the whole neighborhood."

My little companion said nothing.

My mom was home, just like the first time, but this time so were my dad and my sister. My sister, thank God, was too busy watching the latest telenovela, which, if memory serves correctly, was called *Kesef Katlani,* "Lethal Money." My dad on the other hand was sitting in the kitchen reading a newspaper when I came in with Bustan. Both he and my mom paid only a passing interest in my bringing home an Arab with me. I don't even think my mom recognized or remembered him from the last time.

I gave both my parents the same spiel about my little friend: "His brother is in my unit but stuck on guard duty back at the base and I want to give him something," and then my little friend followed me up to my room to fool around for a little while. Bustan, I have to admit, is the only Arab I've ever had sex with, and I'd be serving him an injustice if I didn't add that he was also the best person I have ever had performing between my legs. He had soft lips and a talented tongue and I could have easily stayed in my room and done more with him, but I felt odd with my parents downstairs below us.

"Wait a second, wait a second," I stammered as I gently moved him, prying my penis out of his mouth. "We need to go somewhere if we want to do this."

Clearly, Bustan was disappointed that I didn't let him finish. He wiped his mouth with the back of his hand and asked, "Can I smoke in here?"

"You can smoke outside." I pulled the socks off my feet and slipped into a pair of sandals. "Let's go."

I led him out through the front door of my house to avoid having to go through the kitchen. I didn't want my parents or my sister to see us. I didn't want anyone to see us, especially that local gossip maven Orlah, but she was standing on her front porch talking loudly on a cordless telephone when we came out. I distinctly remember what she said into that phone: "Listen, I have to go *now*," and I remember seeing her glare at the two of us as we walked past her house. I didn't say anything to Bustan, and he didn't say anything to me, but I did notice him looking at her curiously.

We crossed to the other side of the road and came up to a green house. The front door of the house opened suddenly and this kid I knew named Gidon came bounding down the front steps out to the sidewalk. He practically jumped in front of us, blocking our path.

"Hey Dudu," he said to me, "how's the army?"

Gidon and I had known each other during high school. He was a year younger than me, and, to cut another long uninteresting epic saga short, he and I had fooled around a little bit about a year earlier. Gidon was the first guy I had ever done anything with, and, I must admit, he wasn't terribly good. Gidon, I'd learned the hard way, was also an obnoxious compulsive pathological liar and I didn't like him; I don't think I'd ever really liked him. I've never considered him a friend and there were many times in the past when I tried to avoid him.

Gidon looked the skinny Arab kid up and down and asked me, "Who's your little friend?"

"His brother is in my unit back at the base. I have to give him something."

"Yeah," Gidon asked, "like what?"

"Like none of your business, Gido." I'd made it a habit to intentionally drop the N from the end of his name because he'd told me once that it annoyed him. "We have to go now." I moved past him.

"Where are you going?"

"Away from here, Gido."

Gidon asked, "Can I come?"

"No, Gido. Just go back inside," I told him. "Go home."

We moved away quickly, leaving Gidon standing alone out in front of his green house. I glanced over my shoulder and could tell he was upset. He pouted for a moment before he ran back inside like a disgruntled little child.

I took Bustan down to one of the new houses being built on the northern end of the moshav. It was about five thirty in the evening, and I knew that the construction workers, many of whom were Arabs, ironically, were all gone for the day. It would be possible for the two of us to have some good, hopefully uninterrupted, gay sex, especially once the sun went down. But we were horny and we didn't wait for sunset. Instead we just went down on each other, but then Bustan dropped his blue jeans and grabbed his ankles.

"I want you to fuck me real hard," he said, "with that *Jew* cock."

His words would have been sexy, if he hadn't *spat* the word "Jew." It's a simple, three-letter, monosyllabic word, a label in my case, but his tone added some obvious weight to it. He'd sounded angry, if only for a second, and I entertained a series of choices about what I should do. A small part of me wanted to be offended, but a bigger part of me didn't want to put my dick back in my pants.

I made a choice and fished a condom out of my wallet and slipped it over my shaft. I grabbed Bustan's skinny little waist and impaled him. The boy probably wanted me to ease into him slowly and gently, but I dove in.

Bustan breathed heavily and started moaning. He reached out and pressed his palm against the bare concrete wall while pushing his pelvis into me, forcing me deeper inside of him. I leaned over and breathed hot air down the back of his neck.

"You like that Jew cock in your ass?" I asked him in Hebrew. "Do you like that *Jew* cock?"

This skinny Arab kid groaned. *"Schwayeh, schwayeh, enta so jaiyaneh."*

Translated into English this means "Slow down, it kind of hurts." But I don't speak or understand much Arabic, and even if I had, it wouldn't have mattered. I grabbed the back of his neck and held onto him, totally getting into what I was doing. I suddenly started singing, *"Oseh shalom bimromav, hu ya'aseh shalom aleinu . . ."* I sang this religious Jewish song, gasping at the top of my lungs, and heard the echo of the Hebrew liturgy bounce off the concrete walls.

In that instant I felt Bustan stop thrusting his pelvis back into me. I don't think he liked that I sang that particular song, and he turned his head around to glance at me over his shoulder.

"You must to slow down," he pleaded with me. "You must to slow down."

I didn't slow down. Not at all. I just went right hammering into him until he arched his back and cried out in undeniable ecstasy. We came together, and I held myself inside of him, breathing in and out, draping my tired torso on top of his sweat-covered back.

"Well . . ." I coughed and cleared my throat as I pulled out of him. "That was fun." I took a step back and yanked the condom off my declining erection.

"Yeah." Bustan grabbed the waist of his blue jeans as he stood up straight. "You fucked me real hard."

In the postcoital aftermath of our early evening activities, I smiled at him wisely and said, "I sure did, didn't I?"

"Mmm." The Arab boy put a cigarette between his lips as he buttoned up his blue jeans.

"Have you ever been fucked by a Jew?"

He lit his cigarette and looked at me, his face partially covered by a shadow. "I'm always getting fucked by Jews."

Like any good Israeli, I tossed the sticky condom into a corner and asked him, "What do you mean? Are you talking politics now?" I watched Bustan roll his eyes.

"Who's talking about politics? You asked me a question, I gave you my answer."

"Well," I said as I pulled up my pants and buckled my belt. "I'm just asking since you're the one who brought it up."

"I didn't say anything about politics." The skinny little Arab kid exhaled a cloud of smoke. "You did."

True, I was the one who brought it up, but still, I asked him, "Yeah, but surely you have an opinion, don't you? You're an Israeli."

He shook his head. "Just because I have an Israeli identification card doesn't make me an Israeli. I'm an Arab."

"Yeah, but you're an *Israeli* Arab."

"Yeah, well." He was unmoved. He threw his burning cigarette out the open window. "That's what you say, but does it really make a difference?"

"Should it?"

The skinny Arab kid gave my question a small iota of thought before he shook his head. "No, I don't think it should, not if you just want to fuck me." He stared at me for a second. "That is all you want from me, isn't it?"

"I . . . uh . . . I don't know." I hadn't expected that kind of a question. "Maybe we could do more than fucking."

"Sucking?"

I nodded my head once. "We could do more of that."

He raised an eyebrow and said, "Sure, but next time, don't bring up all this bullshit. Politics bore me. I never watch the news."

Suddenly, right at that very second, a beam of light appeared between us. It quickly spanned across the concrete wall, illuminating my face in the early evening darkness.

I heard Orlah's crotchety old voice. "What the hell is going on in there?"

Orlah was shining a flashlight through a glassless window, lighting up the whole room, nearly catching the two of us in the ultimate act of Israeli-Arab union. Without even thinking, I grabbed the skinny Arab kid's wrist and pulled him down in a squatting position near the floor.

"*Nu?*" said Orlah, shining the beam of light into the house. "I know someone's in there. I heard voices. I heard singing."

The old nosy neighbor of Metzitzah was on to us and, judging by my gut instinct and the look on Bustan's face, I could tell we both knew it. I watched the light wander over the bare concrete walls and saw it sparkle in the reflection of cum drops sprinkled across the bottom of the wall and the floor around us.

"Whoever's in there," Orlah said, "you know you're not supposed to be in there. I'm going home to call the guard, and I'm locking my door." Orlah stopped to give way to a pregnant pause. She probably thought one of us would respond to her or something, but neither of us uttered a word. I tried to take in measured breaths, hoping to further conceal our presence at the construction site. "I'm leaving now,"

Orlah told us, "and don't you *dare* follow me. I've got a gun and I know how to use it, I was in the Haganah."

I rolled my eyes when I heard her say "Haganah." It was the name of a Jewish prestate militia that fought in Israel's War of Independence, and Orlah was forever telling all the people on the moshav, especially the kids, that she'd served with them back in the 1940s. It had become her trademark claim to fame in life, but for everyone in my social circle back then, my friends and neighbors in Metzitzah, it had became the joke about Orlah: "I was in the Haganah."

A few seconds later we heard Orlah make tracks in the dirt gravel as she walked away from the house. I snuck a peak around the jamb of a door to check that she had left, and then I gave the all clear to my little companion.

Bustan brushed concrete dust off the knees of his blue jeans and said, "I'm going to leave now."

"Right." I nodded. "That's totally understandable."

"Yeah." Bustan started toward the wide open door at the back of the house.

I followed after him. "You want me to walk down to the gate with you?"

"No."

"Oh." I could tell he was annoyed. "Okay then. Well, can I call you?"

"Yeah, sure" he said flippantly, "do what you want."

I watched him slip out through the back entrance and then I asked him, "Will you be on the *sherut* next month?"

He stopped suddenly and waited a split second before he turned around and came over to me standing just inside the concrete archway. "I've been riding on that taxi to and from Dirhana twice a week for the past month hoping to see you again. I just didn't think we'd end up in a place like this so we could just fuck." He said, "I don't want to do it here," and nodded his head to the house. "Next time we fuck we must to do it inside some other place, where we won't be bothered."

"Yes, of course."

"Right," Bustan said, "well, you've got my number." He turned on his heel and started walking away from the house.

That was it. I watched him as he walked to the edge of the moshav and moved along the inside of the perimeter fence. For a brief, flickering moment I was reminded of being stuck on guard duty. He lit a cigarette and disappeared somewhere along the horizon, backlit by the crescent of the setting sun. Once he was beyond my line of vision, I slipped out of the construction site and scurried back to the house. Two days later I returned to the base.

Another month passed, however, and I found myself once again on my way home from the army clad in my Israeli fatigues with a duffle bag and the same M16 as before hanging over my shoulder. On the inland road west of Haifa I climbed up into another shared taxi, this time only half full, with a healthy mixture of Israelis and Arabs. Even the driver was an Israeli Jew. But, unlike the last two times I'd done this, my skinny Arab friend was mysteriously absent.

I took out my cell phone just as the *sherut* started along the road and found Bustan's number in my phone book. I pressed the send button. Three, four, five rings later, the voice mail picked up. I listened to the message, half in Arabic, half in Hebrew, and heard the beep before I clicked the end button and closed my phone. I imagine I was nervous about calling him, but I was more worried that he wouldn't remember my name. If I had to remind him who I was, I might have to go into explicit details while my fellow taxicab riders listened.

At the junction for the road to Metzitzah I stepped down out of the taxi and started walking up the road to my moshav alone. I passed by the guard at the gate. He smiled and waved at me through the window.

"What's up?" The guard came out of his little shack and asked me, "Where's your little friend, Dudu?"

Because we all lived together in this tiny community, I knew the guard personally but I didn't like him. His name was Nir and he was also Gidon's father. I'd never liked him. Actually, I kind of hated him.

I acted dumb and asked him, "What are you talking about?"

"You know what I'm talking about. Don't be stupid, boy." Nir grinned and shook his head slowly. "We know all about your little friend." He laughed slightly before he went back to his post.

I ignored him and kept on walking up the main road into Metzitzah. Everyone was home when I got to the house. Our car and two other cars, one for each brother, were parked outside. I went into the kitchen and saw my mom sitting at the table with Orlah.

That old bitchy windbag was going on about something, "The police still haven't found my *tus-tus,* but they say they believe they've caught the little shit Arab who came in here to steal it." Orlah turned to me and said, "Those fucking Arabs, we should round them up and send them to Syria. They're nothing but trouble."

I looked to my mother and asked, "What are you talking about?"

"Someone stole Orlah's scooter."

Orlah piped, "Some little shit Arab came in here and ran off with my *tus-tus.*" She turned to my mom and quieted her voice to say, "And that asshole Nir down at the gate, he said he didn't see anything. He was probably sleeping while he was on guard duty the night it was stolen. That's it." Orlah held up her hands. "Metzitzah needs a new guard."

"Someone stole your *tus-tus?*" I pouted for Orlah. "That really sucks."

"The police can't get him to admit to anything," Orlah added, "even though I saw him outside my house." She glared her beady eyes at me. "Twice."

I understood her silent implication. I tried to act cool as I asked her, "The police already have someone?"

Orlah nodded proudly. "I called them the very second I discovered it was missing."

"When was that?"

"Yesterday morning." Orlah looked at my mom and shook her head. "I had to walk all the way to the Kolbo. Can you imagine a woman at my age walking two hundred meters to the local market?"

My mom shook her head and said, "It's terrible."

Orlah glared at me again with her two beady little eyes. "Isn't it, though?"

I said, "Yeah, it's a real travesty of justice."

"The police have a suspect," Orlah added happily, "he just won't admit that he stole it. But I saw that boy here." She turned to me and pointed. "With you."

"Who?" I asked.

"Oh, you know," replied Orlah, "that little Arab shit that came in here with you. He's the one."

"How do you know that?" I remembered the spiel I'd used with my parents. "His brother is back in my unit at the base," I lied. "That little kid isn't an Arab."

"Oh yes he is," argued Orlah, "he's nothing but a shit little Arab. The police picked him up the same day I called them. They found him down at the junction waiting for the taxi."

"And he had your *tus-tus* with him?"

"Well . . ." Orlah paused. "No . . . but that doesn't mean he didn't steal it."

"How do you know he stole it?"

"*Nu?*" Orlah shrugged her old lumpy shoulders. "Why else would he come in here?"

I saw the light of inner doubt flash across her dark eyes. "You don't know that he stole it though, do you?"

"He's an Arab and was here when he shouldn't have been." She turned to my mom. "That in and of itself should be a crime."

"Well, I disagree," I said as I opened the refrigerator to take out a bottle of juice. "Besides, if we're talking about the same person, I'm telling you, he's not an Arab."

"Your friend," Orlah asked me, "the one that was here, his name was Bustan, wasn't it?"

I closed the refrigerator slowly with all the tension of being caught in a lie. I turned to my nosy neighbor slowly and stared at her. I even opened my mouth to speak but no words came out.

"Actually," my mom nodded and said, "that was your little friend's name, wasn't it, David?"

"Well . . ." I stammered silently for a second, "yeah, but that could just be a coincidence."

Orlah shook her head. "No, I don't think so."

My cell phone started vibrating in my pocket. I took it out and saw the number for the incoming call; it was Bustan. "Well I think you're wrong." I smiled at Orlah. "I think it's just a coincidence." I stepped out of the kitchen and went up to my room before I opened the phone and said, "Hey Busie! How are you?"

"Who is this?" was the answer I received. "Who is calling this phone?"

"Who am I?" I asked. "Who are you?" I could tell this was not the Arab boy I was talking to; the voice on the other end of the phone spoke perfect Israeli Hebrew.

"This is the police. Who is this, please?"

"I . . . uh . . . I . . ." I stuttered and sweated, "I'm just a . . . you know." I quickly jammed my finger down on the end button and closed my phone. Then I took the battery off to prevent any further calls from the police. It was obvious to me that something was wrong; something had happened to Bustan. Whatever it was, I knew it was best for me to stay out of it.

I changed out of my uniform and came back downstairs a few minutes later. By that time, Orlah, thank heavens, had left and my mom and sister were setting the table for dinner. My two brothers were sitting in front of the television in the living room watching a soccer match between Maccabi Tel Aviv and Hapoel Beer-Sheva, while my dad, seated in a rocking chair, read a newspaper two days too old.

Suddenly there was a knock on our front door. Everyone in the living room turned to look at me, but not one of them made even the slightest effort to get up out of their seats.

"Don't move," I sighed. "I'll get that."

I came over to the front hall and opened the door.

"Hi there," it was Gidon. "I thought I saw you walking up the road."

"What do you want, Gido?"

"Where's your little friend?" He smiled at me. "He didn't come with you today?"

I stepped out onto the front porch and closed the front door behind him. "No, Gido, he's not here with me. What do you want? Why are you here?"

He grinned at me. "I've got something to show you."

"Like what?"

"Come with me," he said, "and I'll show you."

"I just got home. I don't want to go anywhere with you."

"Oh come on." He winked his right eye. "I know you'll want to try it out once you see it."

"Gido . . ." I shook my head slowly, "What do you want to show me?"

"Just *come* on." He skipped down the front steps. "It's cool, you'll really like it."

I rolled my eyes and said, "Fine," and walked away from my house with him, not because I wanted to but because I just wanted Gidon to get away from my house. I really detested him sometimes.

Gidon led me down to his green house and took me around to the back. "This," he said and pointed to a storage unit sitting along the rear of the house, "is something my dad and I put up a few months ago."

I turned to Gidon with exasperation. "You wanted to show me this?"

"No." Gidon grinned and shook his head slowly. "I wanted to show you this." He stuck out his tongue to show me his new piercing.

"Hmm." I nodded noncommittally. "Neat." Nowadays a pierced tongue is nothing uncommon, especially among gay men in Israel, but back then, when I was eighteen, this sort of thing was just starting out as a vibrant, youthful modern trend.

"The thing is," Gidon started, "I haven't had a chance to suck cock since I got it and people say a pierced tongue really helps with the stimulation."

"What's your point, Gido?" In reality, I knew I didn't have to ask.

"I wanted to know if I could suck on your cock and you could tell me how it feels."

I just laughed at him. "You want to suck my cock with that thing in your mouth?"

"Well," he said, grinning and nodding, "yeah."

"Where?" I pointed at the storage unit. "In there I suppose, right?"

Gidon nodded his head slowly and walked over to the double doors. He unlatched the lock and opened the storage unit. "We won't be disturbed in here." He cocked his head in my direction. "Not like the last time you got off when you were home."

My proverbial chin hit the proverbial floor. It seemed as though Orlah had seen me having sex with Bustan, and, in the time I'd been away from Metzitzah, it appeared she'd made the gossip rounds with that little piece of notoriety. I'm willing to bet the whole moshav was well aware of my sexual antics with the Arab boy.

I folded my arms across my chest. "What are you talking about, Gido?"

Gidon shrugged as he stepped to the side of the storage unit. "Come into my office and we can talk about it further."

I stared at Gidon and shook my head before I looked into the storage unit. Inside, the place was an utter disaster, a giant mess. Dirty sheets and tablecloths and cans of paint and long fluorescent lighting fixtures looked as if they'd been tossed in there without any thought.

I continued to shake my head from side to side. "Oh Gido, this will never work out."

"Why not? You had sex in the construction site the last time you were here, what's wrong with this place?"

"It's not the place, Gido, it's the person."

"What's that supposed to mean?"

I let my eyes wander over the mess of the storage unit and something unexpected caught my eyes. One of the dirty tableclothes looked like it was draped over a chair or a seat of some kind. I ruffled my brow when I noticed it and I took a step closer.

"Gido," I said and pointed at the dirty table cloth tossed over the chair, "what's that?"

"What?" He followed my gaze and said, "Oh, that." Gidon quickly grabbed another dirty sheet and tossed it over the chair. "It's nothing. It's . . . uh . . . something my dad is working on."

I pushed my way past Gidon and pulled the dirty sheets and table cloth from the chair. Beneath all that dirty fabric was a *tus-tus,* a scooter, the kind you see old women like Orlah driving around a moshav.

I made an inquisitive face and said, "Hmm."

Gidon stepped in to cover the *tus-tus* with the sheets. "It's not what you think it is."

I said, "It looks like Orlah's *tus-tus* to me." I looked at Gidon with pity. "I guess I shouldn't be surprised with your jealousy."

Gidon hid the scooter under dirty fabric and asked, "So, do you want a blow job or not?"

I raised my eyebrow and sighed.

# ❧ 14        Little Stints

*Desmond Ariel*

They are the *shabbab,* the youth, still full of sap and not yet wasted. They can terrorize the expats. Emerging from once suburbs, now town centers—Al-Sulaymaniyah, Manfouha, Olaya, Malaz—they step out of white-walled villas trimmed with bougainvillea, from just kissing their fathers once, twice, three times, four, on each cheek, and even rubbing noses. They step into Toyotas Cressidas or Chevy Caprices, all gleaming and new, leather and chrome. For the better off, top-of-the-range Lincoln Town Cars, Lexus, Mercedes Benz that shimmer in the light. They lift their pristine white *thobes,* like nightgowns billowing on bronzed flesh. They stretch their legs as they drive around the highways, one hand on the wheel. With the other hand they adjust their headdresses above the forelock, tilted left or right, using finger technique to get the shape right, just so. A tribal allegiance, Shammar or Dawasir, is defined by this dandy style of desert. They cruise the flyovers, the slip roads, the parking areas, the car showrooms; they hold up traffic, doing U-turns too fast, curb crawling to chat to passing friends. Young men, freshly perfumed with sandalwood oil, crunching the accelerator and burning up fuel. Because they can.

The *banaat,* the girls, watch their counterparts from behind veils, behind darkened windows, across screens in restaurants that divide the sexes, or from behind their male drivers. They think of little else but shopping and boys. The swooning is just for show, till they catch one and fill his nightly dreams with their nacreous odors and discreetly drop their telephone numbers. Parents forbid girls to go near boys—for a girl to even look at or talk to a boy is the crime of intercourse. If you kiss one, it is prison, shame, dishonor, even death. Yet,

*Gay Travels in the Muslim World*
© 2007 by The Haworth Press, Inc. All rights reserved.
doi:10.1300/5481_14

illicit thrills lure them on. Girls study boys like they study grammar, do trigonometry, for how to connect dangling participles, solve the X and Y for vital equations. There are ways to slip love messages into cigarette packets, tossed airily out of blackened car windows. They ache to feel the silk of boy skin, to feel what lies underneath the crispy white robes. Their mothers flip at the thought that what their daughters do may go unpunished. Their fathers, meanwhile, reach for a hot branding iron, or even a gun.

The boys talk like landowners, like top cats. People complain—the word *shabbab* often on their lips, but refer to the boys who get too wild. But some expat men, whether homo or just in a phase of marriage fatigue, secretly lust after the young men: some discreetly, some not so. The very daring ones stand on the roadsides waiting to be picked up—guaranteed within minutes. Merely to be out alone is enticement. The real *shabbab* beauties can trifle with a man's desires as easily as they flick cigarettes from car windows, or wink to cousins in a traffic tailback. A date, to them, is a soft resilient fruit that feeds you through hard times. Some boys prize this power to seduce so fast, and take full advantage. Others are barely conscious of it. They smile— sweet water from uncontaminated wells. They charm their way through any encounter with rich or poor, local or foreign. Their presence beams across a balmy sunset I never want to end.

The wilder ones, Martin and Hector say, came from the villages, from Al Kharj, or farther away, from Al Falaj, Wadi Al Dawasir. It is being out on those farms that does it. If you can catch one pure bedouin youth, Hector says in reverent tones of wish fulfillment, they are sexier, less spoiled. The ones in the city already becoming urbanized, turning sour. Martin and Hector groan about this as a cataclysmic descent into the Western, the more grasping, the mercenary. The boys might just ask me to give them something, a gift. Something of mine that they think by rights is theirs. And if I don't, then, well, they might just take it anyway. There's a growing underclass that cares less for the old, gentlemanly ways of the rich and educated Arab.

Some young men, once allowed away from their families, loiter around the dusty, rank, noisy downtown Battha souk. They go bargain hunting, to meet their friends. Ogling the men-only crowd that wanders the nexus of pathways. One guy I encountered—the time escapes me now—exposes his not-insubstantial dick for my viewing. I'm afraid to look in case someone sees, afraid of his boldness where justice is swift and cruel and secret police loiter. It is in the toilet stalls of the Battha Hotel. I look left and right; the lobby well-known to be cruisy, but watched. They guy is slim, tall, and handsome. He has long hair. He spits on his hand, then on to his large tool, to lubricate it, all for my benefit. He makes words useless, winking and gesturing me to join him. I turn to go, but am frozen to the spot, dying to see more as much as to flee.

Hector, once veteran and master of the Battha Hotel scene, loves the car park nearby. He was once fucked on a hidden rooftop there. Wallops of instant lust—a dangerous addiction. He traipses around the souks; crutch-cruising the mass of hungry, darting, charcoal eyes; wandering in and out of stacks of stereos, TVs, displays of gold chains, and swatch watches, as glittery and dazzling as Hindu shrines. Hector would pick a local, or be picked, take him home, get straight to business, dust him off, all patted with talcum on the armpits and butt, and send him back on his way. Then, perhaps, if there is time before supper, consider a second, or maybe even a third. No mere slick-legging for him—the real hole is good and always ready. Hector stops going when it is too risky to be seen there. Warnings go around of a new stabbing, or a police arrest, of murder cases unsolved. Weeks later, he slinks out again when the time is riper and danger subsides, ready for a new catch.

In those early days too, I remember, when Martin and Hector were still around, Battha was flooded with magnificent Yemeni youths, livelier and wilder by far than Saudi *shabbab*. They wore kohl around the eyes, swathed their heads like breadbaskets with confident, insouciant style. Hector called it "the twenty-four-hour, nonstop Yemeni cabaret," which is what it sometimes felt like, till the war meant they were sent back to Yemen. They pursued their chosen ones down the street with the efficiency of a bayonet drill. One chasing me so hard I had to give him the slip. But he caught up. Each time I looked back, he was still there, winking, pleading with me to come with him. He wanted me, at any cost. He'd stop at nothing. He was not unattractive, just scarily persistent. To never take no for an answer changes the rules. For the first time in my life I actually worried about being raped, about being held down and forced.

The Yemeni boys were once leaders of the crowds along Battha corniche—again Hector's amusing name for it, as it was miles away from the sea. The cars however still came in tidal waves. The frantic minibuses like dodgems, honking, rip-roaring. It was a shopping walkway clotted with debris, dust, and merchandise, not a single drop of moisture in the air, always the constant search, the swish of legs and loins, the easy pickings, basting in the electrostatic.

The current youths dodge the crowd of Indians that makes way for them. They are the thorny rosebuds of the merchant classes, the Arabian peninsula's finest. They respect their elders. They praise their teachers—usually Syrians, or Egyptians—for passing them through exams with ease, through every grade like opening a set of stepladders. They have an instinctive aversion to problems. Their true creativity was in avoiding unnecessary action. Their talent, always for the shortcut, for saving face and family honor. Yet, they did take the trouble to shave their pubic hair in the shower, leaving a trail of water on the floor for the maid, or their mothers, or their lovers, to mop up. Someone is there to hand them a towel—always. They only have to reach out. They remember to moisturize their thighs with lanolin. Any salt that gathers around their balls only adds flavor, till the next shower. They practice hard at football, admiring Italy, Argentina, and especially Brazilian players, and their own stars of the field, their own clubs whom they idolize without reservation.

They often tell good jokes without bungling the punch line. Commerce runs in their blood; they can sell you anything—even passion—but violence holds no sway there. They prefer calm to reign. They do not drink alcohol, use swear words, or kiss anyone on the lips unnecessarily. They do not put out their tongues. They move like gazelles across a wide open plain. They rain kisses on the ground with each silent, sandaled footstep, with each throwaway laugh. When they smile, it's the discovery of an unsuspected oasis after days of hardship. Their faces mostly the work of a truly great artist almost getting it right each sketch.

I watch them, sometimes in awe, which inspires dread. To have them and not to have them. I wavered. I think back to the spotted young men of Birmingham. Darrens, Kevins, and Steves, raw, crude, gangling, and broken, whose style is clunking, or inelegant. Brummie boys who curse rather than kiss their fathers—never! Boys too loud, or too sarcastic, who never praise anyone, least of all God, who think that to touch a buddy, to show him any affection is an abomination and too fucking girlish to be true!

How different boys can be here where they hold each other's hands. They always kiss on greeting. They like each other and don't mind showing it. The high-minded among them always read the Koran, criticize the morals of others, worrying their prayer beads, twisting their chin fluff that one day will grow to a fine, imposing beard. These are the ones who fume with an unpredictable, unresolved anger.

Others, the ones I notice first, scratch their balls, dart back come-on glances. Not lewd, but not itching down there either. Just desire, undiluted. Aimed just so, to bed their prey, no messing. The trick is not to look back, to give way too soon. There are plenty. If I look at them, even in nervous reflex, they don't stop their pursuit until it happens. If I don't vanish fast, they track me down so I needed my rabbit hole to run to. But the act, never on the streets, always behind closed doors, retaining the sacred dignity of the public space. The tactics are simple, amusing, deadly. Some car chases for sex go on way into the night, till dawn eventually exhaust me into long-delayed sleep.

One young man I meet tells me he is the uncrowned master of the road, of car-crash city. He's careless of injury. He pulls rank on police who come to arrest him by just mentioning his name. He scorns the stick-waving of the religious police in their hairy-ankle-exposing *thobes*. He becomes, like all the others, just a youth fulminating to his prime, snatching his due, commanding his place in the world. Always among equals, editions of himself. Boys could have, should they want, another of their choice. A Fahd, a Mohammed, an Abdullah, a Feisal, Samir, Khalid, a Sa'ud, an Aymen or Na'if. All so adept at the tangled signals of brief lusts. Sure of an infinite supply, the world providing such plenty that jealousy is rarely spotted. If you lose one, another comes along, juicier, fresher.

The best *shabbab* I think are unassuming, not high and mighty. If they say *"salaam,"* my mind's elevator stalls—my organs shift. If a handsome one says *"habbibi,"* darling, to me, I'd go through a red light just to catch up, to gaze at his soft-toned skin, his bright, wily eyes, and squirming toes, dry-flaked heels. To hear the words come again. To inhale his presence, to taste his fat-crackling laughter, I learn perhaps that he's trained in tae kwon do, loves rap music, has been to Tampa, Florida, knows the ins and outs of the stock exchange, shaves his pubes, can fix a four-wheel drive, yet still has his hint of sandalwood smoke; tales of desert genies; honey tobacco; his cool, bored, devastating purity; the desert dew etching the ghost of a mustache across his lips.

True, some guys I met talked about girls as they make love to me. Like I am their substitute for the absent female. This is not strange in any way. The beauty of a marriageable girl, her precious cherry-prize taken for granted, sniffed around, as rightfully theirs, not ever in doubt. It's no stain on their manhood to be in bed with a boy. The duty of girls preordained as future mothers of future sons. But the closer I look, some of them—at first not many, but then more and more, also like the beauty of boys. Sons above all others—their mothers agree and adore them for life, even above their husbands. A son is their one true love who is theirs forever; but a husband might find a second or third wife, discarding the first.

To get in and get out of a bedroom unobserved is the trick, to avoid afterthoughts. Some even had sex with their clothes on. One called Souleyman—I met him in a supermarket—insisted that the real bedouin never take their clothes off to make love. He pulls out his erection, but the *thobe* stays on. They do it behind rocks, he said, squatting, predator wary. The antidote to romance. No time for the delicate art, the paraphernalia of love. No feel for reciprocity. They want to fuck, then wash, then go. People then blanched from their minds. Another one amazing me with sexual tricks I could not possibly have imagined, showing a technique beyond his twenty-five years. Some partial to older men, not ageist at all, seeing older men as sexual prey.

Martin astonished me one day by declaring "They lack the vocabulary of intimacy." But maybe we lack something they have too.

\* \* \*

One day, another, then another. I spent a great amount of time away from any British or American expats. The worst period was where I wanted to forget who I was, for which I felt perfectly situated, as I didn't live in a compound, or have people asking what I was up to. I felt they did not understand why I preferred the company of locals, getting to the essence of *shabbab* through their dicks. I turned to sex for solace and indulged in these wayward youths.

They became a fix for my down moods. They added to the monotony of the desert city, but relieved the longeurs all the same. I needed them to get by like recognizable blips on the sea of dunes. They came to visit me at the flat, an endless round of nameless, fine-chiseled faces, surreptitiously asking if anyone else was in before they dared enter. Not one like Yussef, never one.

The first one to phone me that evening was called Mohammed.

He asked if he could he bring his uncle. I agreed and waited for two to turn up, but when he opened the door, there were three of them standing all in a row, each one slightly smaller than the other, like matching ornaments on a mantelpiece.

"This is my friend, Samir. This is Khaled, my uncle," Mohammed said. Mohammed walked in, kicked off his sandals and relaxed on the sofa. The other two followed suit. Mohammed flicked the remote to the sports channel. There was a football match on and he followed every move of the players in his team. He roared even when there was no goal.

I nodded and sat opposite the three of them looking at them. They smiled at me; I smiled back.

The phone rang. I answered it.

A dusky voice said, "I am Mohammed. *Salaam.*"

"*Salaam Aleikum.* Hamed or Mohammed?"

"Mohammed."

"Which Mohammed do you mean? The fat one from the Car showroom or the tall one from the supermarket that has a BMW? Do you have a brother called Samir who keeps scorpions?"

"No," said the voice, "I don't keep scorpions."

"Not you. His brother." I restrained my growing annoyance. "My brother doesn't keep scorpions. You know me."

I had no idea who he was so put the phone down. It rang again. I ignored it and went to the kitchen to get the snacks. I heard them discussing what they wanted to do with me from the kitchen. When I walked back in, they stopped.

The day before I'd received yet another call from someone claiming he had met me in Bahrain, mentioning his full name and details of the room and hotel, but no jogging could help me recall that person, or whether anything had happened between us. I struggled, but I could not recall a thing. Was the guy lying? I hoped something would remind me soon.

"Can I use the phone?" said Mohammed beginning to dial. "I have to phone my cousin."

"Go ahead. Please."

While Mohammed was busy on the phone, I turned to Samir and Khaled. They were smiling at me again, knowing they'd come to the right place.

I somehow knew Khaled from somewhere. "Haven't I met you before?"

"I don't know," said Khaled, "but my cousin says he knows someone like you."

"Really? What's his name?"

"Khaled," he said, laughing, "Just like me."

I recalled another Khaled I'd once met, who had had long hair until he became an army cadet and shaved it off. He looked very good bald. The Khaled sitting next to me on the armchair looked the spitting image of the other—it was uncanny but not uncommon.

Khaled lit a cigarette and said, "Have you got any whisky?"

"No, I don't like whisky; makes me feel sick."

Khaled and Samir both looked at me as if he were lying, or insane.

"Okay. Give me Coke," Khaled said.

I fetched two Cokes and put them on the coffee table. I opened each can and gave one to Khaled and one to Samir.

"Ashtray," said Mohammed.

I went out to the kitchen to bring an ashtray and put it down next to the cans of Coke. I didn't want to smoke myself yet, as I was trying to give up.

Mohammed knew some English, but Khaled and Samir couldn't speak any, and they looked at me, amazed to hear it spoken by a real foreigner. They turned their heads to Mohammed for a translation, even when I spoke Arabic.

Mohammed put his hand over the phone receiver and held it out to me.

"Just talk to my cousin for a minute. He wants to have you."

"Really?"

The voice on the phone was nice, friendly. He spoke passable, if broken, English. He was in a good mood.

"So, hello. What's your name?"

"Samir," said the cousin.

"That's funny," I said, "we've got a Samir right here. Do you know each other?"

It turned out that they had been to the same school. Sometimes I strained to match names to faces. I never liked to forget, in case I'd also met him before, as I myself would not want to be forgotten.

"Don't tell him anything about me," said Samir in Arabic. He turned to Mohammed next to him on the sofa in alarm. "Mohammed, tell him not to say anything."

"Hey mister," said Mohammed, "Don't say anything about my brother, will you?"

"No problem. I won't."

I turned my shoulder toward them and carried on talking.

"So what can I do for you, Samir?"

He wanted to come right over, but I said no, it would have to be another time. I was entertaining guests. But I knew someone who might be interested in taking my surplus visitors. He only had to call back later, but of course, he wouldn't.

Khaled, Samir, and Mohammed finally decided to take it in turns by age. If they weren't all going to go together with me in the room—and that had been known—one had to volunteer to go first. The blinds were closed; the lamp turned downward, pooling light up the wall behind the bed. First came Mohammed, being the eldest. There was not a scrap of fat on his naked body; the meat was all weighted firmly in the cock. His nose was symmetrical, his expression fixed, except for the eyes. He was very assertive and intense. His trouble was that he came too quickly. Didn't even wait to get it in. He got overhyped with talking, and then it was all over. Delaying tactics did not work. I lay on the bed and watched him go out.

Next, Khaled, Mohammed's uncle, came in. Khaled was better. He had not washed that day, but his odor was good, it was earthy, salty, but still clean. He had hair on his arms and legs. His balls were small, but he didn't turn his head away from a kiss, though he would never open his mouth fully. He had rhythm in his pelvic thrusts. He made noises, but his each of his hands did different things, went in varying directions. I wanted to tell him to slow down. When he stroked my back, it was forced and clumsy, as if he were touching something that he couldn't sense through fingertips, that wasn't alive. It could have been a cupboard or an egg box. Samir was watching us through the gap in the door. When I got up, standing naked in front of him, and asked him to join us, Samir backed away, pretending he was looking for his baseball cap. He wouldn't come in while Khaled was there—he would wait, hovering at the slightly open door, touching his dick.

I clicked the door closed. Khaled then turned over and said, "do it to me, but don't tell them, *w'allah,*" I said okay and I enjoyed myself with Khaled, who enjoyed every minute too.

Once Khaled had finished, he went very quiet. He stood and looked out of the window and lightly brushed the sperm from his dick. In profile, his nose and cock were out of proportion to his body. They were both large on his skinny frame, so he had the arched look of an elegant flamingo standing on one leg in a pond.

"Bathroom?" he said. Then, he followed my finger, and with a towel wrapped round, falling off his ass, he slipped into the bathroom. I heard the water gush out of the showerhead onto the enamel.

Mohammed, now dressed, was talking on the phone. Khaled was having a shower, with the door open. Samir came into the bedroom. He wasn't as pretty as Mohammed, but he was much more sensitive.

He took his time to establish a sensual mood. He asked where he could hang his robe, and as he was putting it carefully on the clothes hanger, Khaled walked in, the tiny hairs on his soft thighs still wet from the shower. He looked very confident, like a distance runner waiting for a medal. He picked up his things, not even looking at Samir and me.

I decided to check the other two first. Mohammed and Khaled, smiling, slapped each other's palms. Khaled sat down on the sofa, beaming, his cock peeking from under the red towel like some curious rodent nosing out of its nest.

I slipped the latch down. I'd concentrate on Samir. At first, Samir just lay there, wooden, unmoving, waiting for something to happen. He didn't budge at all until I massaged his upper chest, and found his cock already hard, bursting out of the opening in the thin cotton. My hands slid under the cotton, and Samir twitched, slipped out of his shorts and lay back down in the same death pose. Samir wanted to kiss—to me just a light brushing of the lips, tongue withheld. He didn't want the others to know, so he kissed me as though he was licking a stamp for a letter whose address he didn't know. I pushed Samir's dick between my legs. I didn't want to bother with the full thing. Even so, it was over in five minutes.

No one had fucked anyone. Three were happy, one was not.

When they had all gone and I had showered, I sat thinking that I was turning into a service station: What to do?

I was suddenly famished. There were three hours to kill before I would go to bed. Sleeping would be even more difficult. I flicked noisily through my diary, full of names. I wasn't about to do serial sex in a big way like others did to fill time, I was just empty and curious. I remembered most of the names, or thought I did. One scribble reminded me of a young guy I'd met in a gym. It was not Mohammed; it began with A but I couldn't remember the rest; the writing was indecipherable.

I stared at the number for a while, closed the book, opened it again, and dialed. A dark mumbled voice spoke, "Alloo."

I explained who I was and where we'd met. The voice agreed: it had all happened exactly as I said.

"Can you come over, say in half an hour?" I said. "Remember where I live?"

"Yes, but just tell me again."

I explained again. Then I sat and waited. I drank two Cokes, flicked through some books, watched the next football match, wondering if I'd slept with any of the players.

They were always late for any appointments—or they never turned up at all. Finally, the doorbell rang. I was tired and on edge. I opened the door just as my neighbor, the nosy Egyptian from the office, was passing. He stared right into my room, at the disarray on the table. He glided on down the corridor. I could not speak—the young man at the door was not the one I thought was coming. I had no idea who he was. This one was not so handsome, having a flabby look. He was eager to step in before I changed my mind. Sometimes that didn't matter, I was glad of the company, as long as they behaved well, but he had a very sad face, heavy bags under the eyes, and was a little overweight. I felt tired. I did not wish to do charity work, or to be reminded of the silence in my room again.

"Did we speak on the phone? I met you in the gym?"

"Yes, I am the one," he said, grinning.

"Are you sure?"

He stepped forward, but I held the door tight. It was a trick. This was an imposter.

"Oh, I'm really busy right now. I have to go out," I shook my head, pushing the door to. "Sorry."

I memorized the features to avoid a repeat scenario. The voice had sounded like the other one for sure. The man looked panicked as his chance for sex began to elude him.

"My brother is busy. No problem I come now?"

Brother or no brother, it was just not the same. I felt the day I would not care about such differences grow closer, and I felt I had to stop.

"I am Mohammed," he said, pushing in again. I stopped him.

"Sorry Mohammed. I have to leave now. Call me tomorrow."

Even in my head I made an excuse. I would not be at home for days. But he might turn up at any time unannounced, the danger being he now knew where I lived.

"Tomorrow? Okay. Tomorrow," said Mohammed looking lost, but smiling as if this date were arranged and all would be well the next day. He then went down the corridor, every other step a slight skip.

I leaned against the closed door feeling numb but relieved. Normally at this time I'd feel restless and go for a drive to exhaust myself before going to sleep. But I was sick to sleep. Sometimes I passed by Martin's old house and wished he was still there. His letters from Yemen were getting infrequent. Sex was just something people did with their bodies, I reminded myself. The candidates tended not to vary that much—they'd even send their brothers in their place. I usually supervised the social peripheries (very basic), the entrance (very clumsy), the culmination (very quick), and the aftermath (very wet bathroom floor) but that was all of it. It was a film I'd seen a dozen times. I knew the opening credits, the lead-in to main action, and finale by heart. I strived to notice any nuances in this sequence. Then I even stopped looking for those and took in only the sensory data.

I had managed not to think of him the entire evening—even for a whole week. I sank into the armchair. Slowly, my forehead arced down, tapping the coffee table surface, knocking the empty cans and ashtray to the floor.

"Yussef. Yussef. Yussef."

\*   \*   \*

Days later, I went to the new square. As far as my eye could see was this new building, vast and geometric, its rectangle replicated down to the last detail of the gutter stones in a zigzag motif. When I looked closely, however, it was rigidly symmetrical. This area was formless, high and rocky but flat, with angular wedges of rock. Each house was surrounded by a high wall, each window was small and never faced out across to another house. There was a long, wide road, which looked white from a distance, leading to the square. A regimented line of palm trees gave shade.

Some of the marble and the inlaid stones were fake. The entire complex had been created to house an idealized group of families. There was rarely any movement from anywhere, except the waving of the palm fronds as they sizzled, clacked, and swished against one another in the wind. The houses even had furniture, just no life. Pristine and remote, the area perfectly suited my mood. The quiet crept upon me so I sat very still, to not resist.

Occasionally, I saw a figure in a dirty pink robe and embroidered skullcap. There was only ever the one—a Sudanese guard. To have looked in the guard's direction would be to invite his curiosity. I ducked behind a palm tree. I didn't want anybody coming up. It was not marked as private property, but that didn't stop guards from challenging my right to be there.

Yussef and I used to sit on this very bench, bathed in the deep indigo shade of a palm tree. The curling fronds looked like grasshopper legs stretching down. I would sit and watch him walk toward me from the car park. At first he was just a tiny red-and-white blotch approaching me from way back in the hot dust haze. I swatted flies that buzzed lazily around my eyelashes. His outline would become more defined, like an incremental line traversing a graph, soundless and dry. Yussef's walk struck me as odd. It appeared to go backward, as though he was moving away, not toward me. He came closer gradually, face visible. Yussef would stop to smile first, tilt his sunglasses up to get a better look at me. The smile annexed his entire face. He'd step up to the bench. I'd leap up from the bench, also smiling. We'd embrace and kiss, Arab style.

"What are you doing here?" he'd say.

"Joker. I've been waiting."

"It's not good to wait too long."

"Then get here earlier."

"Let's go then."

We'd go back slowly across the square, talking.

I could remember the exact sound of the voice, its soft inner quality, its coppery warmth. Following the line of palm trees for shade, we'd become engulfed in the building's massive, axial design, its main blocks posed high above others, seemingly unsupported, its massive slices of shadow and sun, in its towering, sterile climaxes. We'd be pin pricks in that scene. Sometimes we'd just drive around, and he'd bring me back to my car.

Now though, with Yussef long gone, there's only the feeling of no people around. I wanted it to be complete, satisfying, with its bored, pleasurable fatigue intact. I sank down slowly on that bench under the palms. My eyes closed. To doze off one could feel years pass in seconds. When I woke, he was still not there, only me as usual.

I tried reciting poetry from memory. That had worked for a while. Then I stopped. I tried listing my favorite books and films. But that was tiring too. They tended to fade with time. Maybe I also just needed water, or even better, a good fresh cocktail, so hard to come by. I walked across the stones, losing count. I felt light, like a cloth blowing on a line, with no bones or flesh. I could smell and hear the trickle of untreated water running from the small irrigation pipes at the base of the palm trees, and this made me want water. I hoped always never to bump into anyone, to allow him or her to disturb me. Once it filled up with people, this empty square became like any other place, littered and abused, its magic lost. When the sun went down over the buildings behind me, they glowed in a teal shimmer, a pale-peach fuzz, each edge and line distinct yet also ethereal. There was no one there to see it at night, as I discovered.

I had heard of a woman, a nurse in a hospital. Louise? Tracy? What did it matter now, she was from England, maybe even from my hometown. She'd had an affair with a married man. It hadn't worked out. One day she went to the roof of her apartment building and jumped, her equivalent of stoning herself to avoid obliging others with the trouble. Other nurses around the pool double blinked at the falling body. They raised the alarm.

This wasn't the only case. There was another, a woman who slid off her balcony during sex. Unless the rumors had been embroidered. She and her lover suggested they oil up their bodies and do it on the balcony al fresco. They must have used a lot of oil. She may have gotten into an arched back position, or where one leg was over the ledge. Then one of then, or both, lost balance. Tugging was useless as limbs slipped through hands that tried to save her. She fell to her death. I recalled this now passing the hospital, as Yussef had suggested we do the same. Sex on his roof his under a star-filled sky. But we luckily forgot the oil.

Sometimes I sighted someone who looked like him. And I got the uncanny feeling he may be still alive and incognito. I saw the back of a head. It looked just like him. The same car. I changed lanes to follow it, to get closer. I tore around corners in this fruitless chase, my heart burning along with the tires. It was always a disappointment to finally pull up at the lights to get a glimpse and realize it was not him at all. Some plainer face sat there smiling. I would feel drained, suffering incurable hope. The entire car chase recycled in my mind before I could sleep. How many replicas of Yussef were there riding around in pickup trucks unknown to me?

*       *       *

I went to Jeddah for a short break. To be near the Red Sea. It isn't overwork, just exhaustion from all the bullshit. Everyone needs to get away and forget it, take a week out to vegetate. The youths are the same there on the coast, perhaps more Westernized. They prey on me, and I on them: the hunters and the hunted. I don't know anyone there. My hotel is on Medina Road. A nice room, plain walls. A view over the highway. I don't usually encourage conversation with people, trying to be faceless. Unless they are.

In the car hired at the airport, I drive around the city, along the endless corniche, on the beach road, to the shopping malls, the kiddies' playgrounds, the statue constructed of cars, the people picnicking on any available grass, past restaurants, hotels, car parks, hotels, hubbly-bubbly gardens, more cars. I am attuned to the danger of roads. To the crazies that take vengeance on others behind a wheel. I circle the Hyatt Regency Hotel and see people waiting. For a bus? Taxis? It is a busy place. More crowded than I remember it. It has been years since I've been here.

There is a boy standing there by the *shawarma* chicken sandwich stall. He is wearing a *thobe* that has seen better days. I circle around the boy in the car, trying to catch a glimpse. Who is he waiting for? A brother? Friend? Family? Perhaps a lover? I decide to stop and offer him a lift. After all, if I don't, someone else surely will. No one is looking. I squint and look again and again. Can hardly believe, but it is so.

The boy resembles Yussef, a younger version. It's in the eyes, in the hands, the way he stands. My hands begin to tremble on the wheel as I turn once more and pull up. I have begun to smoke again, after giving up. I have to know for certain, to get a closer look.

The boy's *thobe* is stained with sand and oil along the bottom edge as though he's been sitting on the beach. He ignores me at first. It is ever their way. How can he not know that here is someone who knows him from old? I hope he will feel this recognition as much as I do. I think through the possibilities: maybe a distant cousin, or nephew of Yussef's? Someone he never had time to mention? The unmentioned, the disappeared form a huge group in this country. You can't talk about them at all.

I click down the automatic passenger window and call out to him, *"Salaam sadiiq. Kay fal hal?"* How are you? The boy signals that he's waiting for someone. He registers no interest in me. He looks away. I ask the boy again though, "Come on. Get in. *Y'alla.* Hurry."

The boy pauses, looks in both directions, and in a flash, gets in. We drive around the streets for a while. We sit and have a juice and talk. The boy smokes all my cigarettes so the packet is soon empty. He says he comes from Riyadh. He doesn't live in Jeddah. Strange then, we haven't met before. What is he doing waiting like that? The boy doesn't answer. I don't push for one. We smile. It's a meeting, a new connection in this town where little ever happens. I like the way he looks. The astonishing similarity.

"You are a foreigner?" says the boy.

"I live here."

"No, only foreigners here. You."

"You mean you've never met any? If you came to my country, you would be a foreigner too."

"What?"

"Okay. I'm a foreigner, not a resident. It's okay with me."

The boy definitely brings back past episodes. I keep looking and studying: the eyes, the nose, the hair, even the fingernails. But this version is newly minted, perhaps twenty-two. I never knew Yussef at that age, so it's an even greater pleasure. The same flick-curl is there. The insouciant calm, the ability to just bide his time. To just watch the honey-brown skin. It is difficult to keep my eyes on the road when driving. I ask him, warily, does he want to come back to my hotel?

The boy nods. He actually likes foreigners. He explains his earlier comments. Foreigners don't stay in the country long. Some of them just disappear. They have a lot of money, from the oil. People like him are out of work. Not everyone is rich here.

We drive to Medina Road and park the car. We pass through the lobby. Two men, not a problem. A foreigner and someone from out of town. Fine. No one has seen us before. Women are out of bounds absolutely, and would alert the police. Men are okay. We can be together.

I lock the door behind him as he goes in the room. The boy looks around. He sits on the bed and switches on the TV, fiddling with the remote.

"You can use the shower if you like."

The boy turns his nose. He has a raw smell, but it's one I like. He studies the TV screen, saying little.

I put down my wallet and go to the bathroom to wash my hands of dust and chicken grease. I smell the sharp scent of blue soap.

I sit next to him on the bed and watch him. He then lies back, putting one hand behind his head. He pulls up his *thobe* by the hem, up to his chest in that bored way I have seen before.

"No, keep it on." I say.

The boy shrugs, only slightly puzzled. He pushes it back only lifting the hem. He pulls down his pants instead, and there is his dick. It lies limp and curled in its nest of dark hair. I get on my knees and start massaging it, taking it to my mouth. It has its own rich taste.

The boy is not that stimulated by my efforts, perhaps tired. He looks around at the table, at the clock, at the smart briefcase. He wants another cigarette. There aren't any left. He asks me could I go and buy some? But I'm not about to leave him alone in the room. I call room service, asking them to leave them outside the door, just to knock. The boy switches the channel to foreign news. He switches back to local news, sound full on. It's the usual labored list of VIP names, ministers, sheikhs, and dignitaries, recited ceremonially. The boy seems to get satisfaction, just listening to the monotony of this. So I leave it on loud for him.

He then starts to play with his still exposed dick, casually flipping it back and forth. It grows a little. Then it dies again. I do and say nothing, just watch. He puts it back in his cotton pants.

I shrug and sit down in a chair opposite.

"What can you give me?" he says.

"In what way?"

"I need money."

"How much?"

"Whatever you've got."

I go to the side table and take some cash out of the briefcase. A few hundred.

"More."

"This is all there is!" I shrug. I've been here before, so little lies are needed.

The boy watches my every move now. Sure his eyes are on me, I get up, walk to the bathroom and bring back a large sharp knife. Under the light it gleams, brand new.

He stares at me. I hand the knife to the boy. "Here. Take it."

The boy, uncomfortable, refuses. He sneers, "What are you doing?"

"Use this. Then you can take the money."

"I don't use this stuff," he says pointing at the knife.

I know now he has stopped trusting me. He's one of those who believes all foreigners play tricks, that we don't believe in the same god, therefore we are aliens who come to take sex and money like prostitutes. But he takes the knife slowly, carefully weighing it his hands. He smiles and then picks out some of the dirt from under his fingernails with the tip. He's used to knives and daggers, just not in the bedroom.

"Take off your *thobe* now," I say. "Everything."

He puts down the knife, stands up and peels off all his clothes. Standing naked now in front of the TV, his dick starts to finally get hard. He has smooth skin, a hard stomach, hardly any hair. He is fine looking. This is what I wanted, to submerge into him. He rubs his dick, like he knows this is what I want. He wasn't relaxed before, but some new mode has entered him and he feels excited.

I take off my shirt and jeans and also stand naked. With the knife in my hand, I move over to the tall mirror. I urge him to come and stand beside me there, calm and determined.

"Put on my clothes now."

The boy, silent, but now following orders, takes my underwear and puts it on. I take his cotton pants, and then put on his *thobe*. It is a little short, but still good on me. My jeans look loose on him, and slip over his hips. My shirt makes him look older. I have a little goatee so with the headdress on, I can now, almost pass for an Arab. One that looks like this youth, my lover. He is smiling and stroking his dick, seeing me as himself.

We stand there looking at each other in the mirror, seeing each other afresh. Now it's different, and we have not just exchanged clothes, this is not just a prelude to sex.

I push him to stand in front of me, with the knife in his hands, both our hands holding on to it. He resists a little, but then plays the part. He begins to twig that there's something I have wanted all these years, not to do with him. We stare a little longer, hands pressing harder over the blade. His muscles straining and his excitement visible, wrestling for power over who controls it. For some minutes we stay like this, his heart beating in front of mine.

My breathing gets harder as I release my hand from his and stroke his hair. He takes the knife, pressing it in the air at my image in the mirror. I laugh, just like Yussef used to, and wait, slow and concentrated, for his next move.

# ❧ 15          Last Winter, in Marrakech

*John Champagne*

By the time I land in Marrakech, my new friend Paul is already waiting for me. A French painter who has been coming to Morocco for over twenty years, Paul is a friend of my Parisian friend Jacques, who introduced us just a few weeks before my trip. I'm spending a year in Paris, on sabbatical from my job in the United States as an English professor, and I am curious to visit more of the francophone world. Since Paul's own trip overlaps with mine, he has generously offered to help me negotiate my first visit to Morocco, choosing my hotel, introducing me to his friends, and offering me practical advice such as "Don't eat anything raw or drink any water from the tap, and whenever you take a taxi, make sure it has a meter." A jovial, stocky man who, despite his graying hair and beard looks at least ten years younger than his actual sixty, Paul takes the seat up front next to the taxi driver, and we head toward my hotel.

I'm a little stunned by my first glimpses of the city, struggling to orient myself to a world that appears both familiar and unfamiliar at the same time. Entering Marrakech, you drive through the majestic dusty pink ramparts of the old city, where you are confronted with thoroughfares crowded with cars, taxis, mopeds, bicycles, horse-drawn carriages, and donkey carts pulling everything from boxes of fresh oranges to rusty machine parts. By late afternoon, the streets are filled with people socializing with one another or walking the pedestrian street that leads to the famous Place Jemaa El Fna. Talking to one another in Arabic, veiled women sit on the ledges of the empty mosaic fountains. Some are completely covered from head to foot. Others forgo the facial veil and black gloves, but their heads, arms, and legs are covered. Some are dressed in Western clothes but still wrap their

*Gay Travels in the Muslim World*
© 2007 by The Haworth Press, Inc. All rights reserved.
doi:10.1300/5481_15

hair in a scarf, and still others are dressed as any European woman might. The men wear either Western clothes or a variety of different *jalababs,* a kind of full-length robe, though nearly all of the Arabs are wearing far more clothes than the Europeans. I am here in February, and although it's warm enough for shorts for some of the tourists, it still feels like winter to the locals. Many of the men in fact wear *jalababs* over their Western clothes to protect the clothes from the ubiquitous orange dirt of the streets.

As he drops me at the hotel that first day, Paul asks if I want to spend the afternoon at a traditional Moroccan public bathhouse, or hammam. In Europe, there are two kinds of hammams: those that are actually sex clubs for gay men along the lines of a U.S. bathhouse, and those that are old-fashioned saunas or steam rooms whose customers are primarily straight. The latter are places where a guy can spend a few hours socializing with other men while also getting a massage or simply enjoying the health benefits of the sauna or steam room. Sometimes, men hook up at the "straight" hammams, albeit discreetly.

I assume that hammams in Marrakech, however, are strictly for nonsexual forms of socializing and relaxation, and although Islamic hammams are always segregated, women sometimes visit the baths, too, at a time separate from the men. Having already visited thermal baths in Austria and Italy, I am anxious to see their Moroccan counterparts, which I have read come borrowed from ancient Roman tradition.

My hotel faces a busy pedestrian street in the heart of the medina. Knowing I am a writer seeking atmosphere on a budget, Paul has made a reservation for me at the Grand Hotel Tazi. The hotel is a bit tacky. Each room is different, decorated in a mélange of indoor/ outdoor carpet, cream colored walls splatter-painted with green, and headboards and mirrors in traditional Islamic motifs done up in gaudy contemporary colors. Nonetheless, the hotel has an ambiance that neither an antiseptic branch of an ibis nor the elegance of a restored *riad* can match.

Clearly, though, the Hotel Tazi has seen better days. The television in my room lacks a remote control and yet is placed so high I can barely reach it by hand. The hot water dwindles to a trickle if anyone else is taking a shower, the wood of the bathroom window is warped, and the fabric of the mismatched armchairs is faded beyond recognition. But the hotel is an ideal place for mixing and mingling. Each night, the faux leather sofas of the lobby are crowded with hotel residents—a mixture of smartly dressed young Arabs and scruffy Europeans—joined by locals, and members of the staff. When a soccer match is playing on the television, the hotel's bar is filled with Moroccan men drinking beer, smoking endless cigarettes, and shouting their reactions to the game.

After I get settled into the hotel, Paul returns to meet me in the lobby so that we can walk together to his favorite hammam. Prior to my trip, friends have advised me how to dress in an Islamic country. Don't expose your arms or legs, they suggest. To dress otherwise is disrespectful and will draw more attention to the fact that you're a Westerner. Although I want to do my best to be respectful of the locals, it's immediately apparent that someone as pale as I am will never be mistaken for an Arab, unless I wear a *jalabab*—and even then, I might be suspected of being a German tourist playing at being Marrakechi. As a result, people tend to look at me as I walk through the street.

Whereas some are just mildly interested in a Western tourist—the economy of Morocco depends on tourism, and the events of September 11th have had a negative impact on the industry—others see me as a potential source of income. I am here in February of 2002, only a few short months after the event. Given the poverty, many people in Morocco have several jobs, some of which include street trade: selling cigarettes, packages of facial tissue, illicit drugs, or sex, or offering to accompany tourists to the palaces and museums difficult to locate in the winding streets of an Arab city.

Paul is the perfect traveling companion. As my father would say, Paul really knows how to "shoot the shit." Whenever we go anywhere, he strikes up a conversation with a Moroccan. When someone in the street offers to be our guide—a practice that is illegal in Morocco—Paul laughs and explains that he is my guide and a true Moroccan himself. Even that first day, everywhere we go we seem to run into someone who knows Paul. Some of them greet him with a boisterous "Saddam!" He explains to me that, before his hair started to thin, some of his Moroccan friends insisted that he looked like Saddam Hussein.

At the foot of the stairs of the hammam, we give six durhams, roughly sixty cents, to a weathered old man, who gives us a numbered plastic token and calls up to the masseur. Paul warns me that the hammam is Spartan, nothing like European health clubs or the famous public baths of Prague or Budapest. From the stairs we enter a tile-walled room with a series of wooden benches. Tile-covered cubbyholes for clothes are built into a corner of the wall. For the equivalent of twenty cents, we pay the young man who stands here to guard our valuables. In another corner of the entryway, I notice a man in a bathing suit shaving in front of a mirror. As I absorb the scene, the masseur, a slight, dark man in his thirties, gestures to me to take a seat on the benches to remove my clothes

Paul moves halfway across the room from me, as he knows the man shaving—a tall Arab with a neatly trimmed beard and milk chocolate skin—from a previous visit. Because Paul doesn't speak much English, I struggle to find a way to ask him discreetly in French how I should undress. The masseur gestures again for me to change, and I finally have the nerve to say to Paul, "I'm not in the least modest, but I understand that the rules for public behavior are different here." I've been told that unlike in the West, you never remove your swimming suit at the hammam except to wash, and even this is done discreetly; generally, you do not display your genitals, even to other men. "Should I change beneath my towel?" I ask. Paul nods, and so I struggle to change into my bathing suit without removing my towel. I notice that some men are even more discreet. They wrap their towels around their whole bodies, first putting on their tee shirts before moving the towel down to their waists so that they can change from their swimming suits—most of which are simply cotton bikini briefs—into their dry clothes.

When I ask, *"Ou sont les WCs?"* the masseur, who speaks very little French, has no idea what I am asking. I ask again. Paul eventually overhears, laughs, and points to a series of ceramic stalls whose entrances are covered by a ragged green tarp that reminds me of artificial turf. Inside each stall is a bucket, two footprint-shaped, elevated areas of tile, and a hole filled with urine. I place my feet on the elevated areas and aim for the hole I am assuming is a drain, wondering what you do if you have to move your bowels.

Because we are getting massages, the masseur, who has changed from his street clothes into a bathing suit, guides us personally into the steam area of the hammam. The door of the bathing area is simply a sheet of plastic tarp. In a corner of the room sits a thin man shriveled by age, the sun, and poverty. He is washing himself over and over again, and is the only man in the hammam who is completely naked. The masseur fills buckets from the taps against the wall and washes down the floor. He then gestures for me to lie down on my back. Paul wanders off to talk to some Moroccan friends.

The masseur soaps me up and then massages my chest and legs. I notice men entering and exiting the room. Since it's the hottest one in the hammam, men tend to wash themselves here, stay for a bit, and then move into one of the cooler rooms. Sometimes the men give one another massages, wash one another's backs, or help one another stretch in the moist heat. Eventually, the masseur gestures for me to roll over on my stomach.

I understand that, for a massage to "work," you have to relax enough to let the masseur's hands penetrate deeply into the muscles, and so I close my eyes and try simply to give myself over to the experience. The masseur straddles me, moving each hand down my arm from my shoulder to my wrist, until he is lying on top of me. I wonder if this is normal for a massage in Morocco, since I've never had a masseur on top of me before. When he moves his hands down my back to my waist, he slips them beneath my bathing suit, but I tell myself to relax, as most massages involve this kind of intimate contact.

At some point, however, I realize that the masseur has an erection he is rubbing against me. I simply don't know how to react. My intermediate-level French will not allow me to respond verbally with any subtlety, and this man speaks even less French than I do. I don't want to embarrass either of us by causing a scene. The masseur is obviously poor; the price of a massage is the equivalent of five dollars, and I don't want him to lose his job for what is ultimately just a harmless flirtation. Given the way a hammam works, we are going to be interrupted any minute by someone else, and, sure enough, when another man enters the room, the masseur jumps up off of me and continues rubbing my back. So I neither encourage nor discourage him but try simply to relax. At one point, however, when we are alone, he pokes his erection between my legs, and I grunt disapprovingly. At the same time, I genuinely want to please him. The massage is a good one, not too rough and not too gentle, and it has been months since another man has touched me with this much physical affection.

When my massage is finished, the masseur kisses me quickly on the mouth, a gesture so gentle it surprises me. Much more familiar is the stereotype of the third world top who fucks Westerners without risk to his masculine pride. I wrongly assumed that a poor, uneducated Arab largely ignorant of Western gay culture would never risk something so romantic as a kiss.

The masseur motions for me to rinse myself off with fresh water he has carried to me. I then move into one of the cooler rooms while Paul receives his massage. Throughout the hammam, I begin to notice that a few men touch themselves, some through their bathing suits, some even showing me their erections, but hiding their actions from the other men. I have no idea what I am supposed to do in response. Paul and I are the only Westerners here. I don't know if this provides gay Arab men with a freedom they would not normally express, if I am being solicited for sex, or if this is simply what sometimes happens at a hammam in Marrakech.

Before coming to Morocco I explained to my gay friends that this vacation is not about screwing the third world. I don't have a particular "type." I am attracted to men of all races, shapes, and sizes, but at this particular point in my life I'm not interested in having sex with anyone I don't actually know. The politics of transnational sex are complicated enough that I'm willing to forgo an erotic encounter in Africa. So, although I did in fact find one of the men in the hammam particularly hot, I didn't react to his gestures except to watch him in a way that I hope conveyed that I enjoyed looking. He repeatedly followed me through the hammam, placing himself out of the line of vision of others, and showing me his erection. But even if I had wanted to respond, I had no idea what to do at a hammam. At any moment we could be interrupted by someone else wandering into the room, and I was not sufficiently curious or horny to risk discovering the consequences of being caught having sex in public in an Islamic country.

As I wait for Paul to finish, I peek through a hole in the wall of the hammam to see the blue-orange sky at sunset. All of the buildings in Marrakech are shades of the same dusty-salmon color, and visible from most of the city is the elegant mosque of Koutoubia. Built in 1199, it is known as the Eiffel Tower of Marrakech. At some point, an imam begins the chant summoning men to the mosque to pray. It is difficult to convey in words the disconcerting beauty of this moment.

When Paul's massage is completed, he tells me that the masseur wants to finish my massage. I'm a little leery, as I'm not sure what this entails, but I dutifully follow the masseur back into the warmest room of the hammam and take a seat on the floor. There, he washes my hair and beard for me. His hands are both strong and gentle as he rubs my face, and he finishes the massage by pouring buckets of warm water over me. He then gestures for me to rest in one of the cooler rooms.

I don't know Paul all that well, as I only met him a few weeks ago, but I still wonder why he hasn't warned me that the massage might include a sexual advance. Later, when I explain to him what happened, he seems genuinely surprised. "He's never done anything like that with me," Paul says, "but maybe it's because I normally come here with Moroccan friends." Paul jokes that he's going to come again to the hammam later in the week, without me. He's disappointed that the masseur has never come on to him. I want to say to him that maybe Moroccans actually distinguish between Westerners, that maybe I'm the masseur's "type" and Paul isn't, but I don't know either Paul or French well enough to say this in a way that is joking rather than insulting. Paul is always on the lookout for sex with one of the locals. From what I gather, these encounters sometimes involve money. He does in fact return later in the week, and the masseur asks to follow Paul home, but Paul declines—he's staying in the apartment of a friend, the masseur doesn't really speak French, and the Moroccan tourist brigade will stop and question any Moroccan person seen walking with a Westerner.

In an e-mail home, I try to explain how this sexual behavior could be tolerated. To my knowledge, the Koran does not prohibit sexual activity between men, except when it warns of the sin of Sodom—though, as in the West, what precisely constitutes this sin is a matter for scholarly debate. Public forms of indecency, however, can be punished in Islamic countries. The problem, of course, is the definition of what might count as public indecency, particularly given the difference between Western and Arab notions of both the public and appropriate behavior, as well as contemporary Arab culture being itself a mélange of colonialism and pre- and post-Islamic worlds. I assume that nomadic culture tolerated certain kinds of homoerotic behaviors necessitated by long periods of time in which women were absent. Adding to this problem is the association of gay identity with Western permissiveness and cultural domination. My sense is that although homoerotic contact between men might be tolerated, in an Islamic country, a homosexual identity is much more likely to be seen as offensive to public decency.

That first night, we have dinner where Paul is staying, the apartment of his French friend Alain and Alain's Moroccan boyfriend Nourdine. Alain is currently in Paris but will return to Marrakech in a few days. His apartment is outside the walls of the old city, near several Western-style dance clubs. An aunt of the king owns an apartment in this same building, and I assume that an apartment like this would go for at least a million U.S. dollars. The floors are all of marble, as are the walls of the bathrooms. In fact, this "bachelor" apartment contains two bathrooms, two bedrooms, a kitchen, two "salons" or living rooms—one Moroccan, one French—and a terrace. The kitchen counter is made of granite and the cabinets are hand-painted. The molding of the Moroccan salon is hand-painted, and the room contains a stone fireplace.

Paul doesn't seem to know how Alain makes his money. In addition to Nourdine, Alain has a French lover back home closer to his own age. When Paul and I arrive, Nourdine is already eating, but as soon as he sees us he clears away his food and begins to serve us the vegetable *tagine* the maid has prepared. Paul tells him to join us, but he refuses. Nourdine's French is worse than mine, but he is taking a class two nights a week. The *tagine* is delicious, the best one I eat all week.

I'm not sure precisely what Nourdine does for a living either, though it involves some kind of construction. Thirty years old, he is strikingly handsome, short, with high cheekbones, bronze skin, and a slight but muscular build. He goes to a gym, an activity still fairly rare in Morocco, at least for nonprofessional athletes. At one point I can't help but say to him, "Do you know what a handsome face you have?"

After dinner, as Paul telephones his sister in France, Nourdine watches television, Mel Gibson's *Braveheart* with Arabic subtitles. On the stereo, a French song that includes, in English, the names of several Beetles' hits—"Yesterday" and "Let It Be" among them—plays. Later in the week I notice that some U.S. films are dubbed in Arabic, but the English dialogue remains audible. Nourdine does not seem in the least troubled by the combination of Arab, French, and U.S. culture. When I try to explain to Nourdine the controversy around Gibson's film, its homophobia, he changes the channel, thinking the movie is bothering me.

Over the course of the week, Paul and I settle into a routine. Each day, I shop in the souks, visit a museum or archeological site, or simply explore the streets of the city, while he paints. We meet up in the late afternoon to have drinks and then dinner.

Nearly every time I leave my hotel on one of my daily walks, a different man offers to direct me to the ruins of the two palaces, the El Bahia and the El Badi. He often begins his pitch, in English, with "Do you remember me? I work at your hotel." If you decline the offer, these men sometimes ask you to join them for a cup of tea. The street hustler, the shopkeeper hoping to make a sale, the student who wants nothing more than to practice his English—all will invite you to join him for tea. Often he insists, "Not for money; just for friendship," but at least one such request ends with the man asking me to buy him cigarettes. One night at the hotel bar, a taxi driver gets me to buy him a beer. As we have been talking all night, I don't mind this kind of hustling, but the barman, a friendly and intelligent guy named Abdelgham, whom I simply call Ab, is embarrassed. "That isn't right," he says in French. "If you offer to buy him a beer, fine, but he should not ask you to buy it for him." Paul thinks Ab is not like most of the other men in the hotel in that if he has sex with a man, he does it because he enjoys it. Paul thinks this is what lends Ab the sadness we both think we see in his face; he is someone Paul thinks of as "really" gay, someone who will never fit in to this culture. He is thirty years old and unmarried. I later learn that Paul has in fact had sex with Abdelgham in the past, and when he offered him money, he refused. Paul has been with several of the staff in my hotel, including the electrician and the plumber.

Due in part to the segregation of the sexes in Morocco, I am never propositioned by a woman, as the sight of a woman talking to a stranger would attract too much attention, even in a big city such as Marrakech. But nearly every time I walk from the hotel to the square, handsome young men say, *"Bonjour, monsieur. Ça va?"* in a way that I recognize as more than just friendly. Once, I make the mistake of simply ignoring the question, and then a group of teenagers harass me. *"Ah, cet homme, il est beau,"* they say, almost menacingly, as if I think I am too good for them. It's one of the only moments during my trip when I feel uneasy about being a Westerner here. The next time a young man speaks to me like this, I simply return the greeting and continue walking. Because I never go beyond this initial exchange, I have no idea if these young men are looking for the longer-term security of a lover, the quick buck of the tourist trade, or simply a little fun.

This moment-to-moment bafflement, the necessity of a constant revising, reconsidering, and recalculating of all that I am observing, is what makes my trip so exciting. Marrakech is like a dream: it feels both familiar and strange at the same time. I think I understand its rules, but then something happens to remind me that this is a world I will never really know or be a part of. I am stunned by its beauty, seduced by its sensuality, and yet shamed by its poverty, too. I want to be a "good" tourist—as if being polite can compensate for the brutal reality of a past dominated by colonialism and a present in which everything has a price. But even this seems too simple, for I can't assume that money is the only thing that motivates the Moroccans I meet, or as if they are simply victims of their past. I can't find a language that won't trap me into pity, romance, or historical amnesia.

Although there is almost no such thing as a visible, public gay identity in Marrakech, men interact physically in public all the time, kissing one another on the cheek, dancing together in the Western-style clubs, and walking arm in arm. Though the European gay men I know all gleefully tell me they think that the king of Morocco is one of us, an unmarried man over thirty is unimaginable. Several times during my trip I am asked if I am married, and when I say no I am usually greeted with a puzzled smile. Because nearly all the Moroccans I meet are polite, however, they try to cover their puzzlement with a joke about the pleasure of freedom. The only Moroccan men I meet who have any sense of a gay identity are those who have traveled or studied abroad, those with French lovers, or those who feel themselves to be more strongly attracted to other men than their friends or co-workers are—many of whom might occasionally sleep with a tourist or even one another, and yet would never imagine a life without a wife and children.

One night, as we are walking toward the square, Paul explains to me a peculiarly Marrakechi form of cruising. At night, among the crowds watching the performers in the square, a man will stand with his hands behind his back. Another man then approaches him from behind and presses himself against the first. Paul offers to demonstrate, and, sure enough, an Arab man approaches Paul from behind. Paul dutifully touches the man's dick through his pants as they watch a group of musicians. Eventually, Paul moves away from the man, and we laugh as Paul mouths a French version of "I told you so," but, as the man walks away from us, he gives me a teasing poke in the ass.

The only woman who invites me to tea is a lovely twenty-three-year-old shopkeeper who sells faux Armani, Nike, and Hugo Boss goods. In the shop one night with Paul, I snicker at these phony designer clothes. The clerk overhears me and tries to convince me that they are authentic, but I simply laugh, *"Madame, s'il vous plaît!"* She jokes, "It is Moroccan Armani." Although some of these designers do actually manufacture their clothes in Marrakech, I can see that some of the logos aren't even accurate.

Fearing that I have offended the young woman, I return the next day to apologize. *"C'est n'est pas grave"*—no big deal—she says, and invites me to tea. We switch back and forth between French and English. Saida explains that her father is from Spain and that the family owns three boutiques. I ask why she doesn't wear a veil, and she explains that once she is married, she will; "No one but my husband should be looking at me," she says.

Saida is the only person comfortable enough with me to admit that Moroccans don't understand why the United States would bomb the poor people of Afghanistan. She calls George Bush a monster. Perhaps her candidness is the result of the fact that we are alone in the shop. When I finish my tea, Saida makes me promise to return to say good-bye before I leave. I promise, but the afternoon of my trip home, she has closed for lunch.

I feel it's my duty to tell everyone I meet that many people in the United States support the cause of Palestinian statehood, that we do not condone the unevenhandedness of U.S. policy in the Middle East, and we recognize that our own foreign policy helped contribute to the events of September 11th, as unconscionable as they were. But I have a difficult time explaining this in French. Most people, however, smile and say that they understand the difference between the people of the United States and their government. I feel they are too generous, as if we as citizens are not responsible for our government's behavior. Being members of a democracy requires us to hold our leaders accountable for their actions. I realize that Bush's blanket condemnation, and grouping together, of Iran, Iraq, and North Korea causes both Europeans and people in the Middle East to wonder if we've learned anything about the dangers of our ignorance of other cultures.

The night Alain arrives from France he takes us to dinner. A thin, slight man in his fifties who smokes constantly, he speaks little English, and, unlike Paul, speaks French so rapidly that I sometimes miss what he says. He's brought along his new pet, a tiny Yorkshire terrier named Safir, to accompany us for the evening.

I am wearing a plaid, button-down shirt and a pair of khaki trousers, and I begin to feel a bit uncomfortable. Nourdine is wearing a suit, Paul has put on a blue Nehru jacket, and Alain, a black sports coat. When we arrive at the restaurant, we are shown to a separate building, apparently some kind of private salon. As the staff greets us I realize that I am decidedly underdressed. All of the handsome waiters wear long, charcoal gray jackets with Nehru collars and matching pants, and they move about in such a way that, after awhile, I can no longer differentiate between guests and staff. We are apparently at the opening-night party of a restaurant owned by one of the favorite caterers of the king.

Our waiter is a friend of Nourdine's named Aziz. When he learns I am a film professor, he asks if I know Richard Gere. Paul thinks the waiter is attractive and manages to get his telephone number before the evening is through. But Paul reminds me that one must be very patient in Marrakech.

At dinner we are joined by yet another well-dressed, young Moroccan. An Islamic scholar named Mohammed who can't find a job, he is studying to be a tour guide. Short, dark, and elegant, he wears a navy jacket over a white shirt and white trousers. After a few drinks, I don't mind being underdressed, as I have several factors in my favor: I am younger than most of the European guests, Paul and I are the token "artists," and people in warmer climates tend to err on the casual side.

Mohammed has a French lover, a man Alain's age who owns some hotel properties in Nice and Cannes. He tells me he has never been to Paris, and I wonder if, like Alain, his boyfriend has a French lover too.

The dinner is a disappointment, a buffet of mediocre French cuisine, but the crowd is amusing, a mixture of models, fashion designers, and other members of the French expatriot demimonde. Some of the women are dressed in ways I would have thought completely inappropriate for an Islamic country, their arms, cleavage, and even stomachs exposed, and some of the men wear striped suits that look like a Ralph Lauren fantasy of life on an English country estate. A woman in a bright red leather miniskirt and jacket accompanies a man who would in the past have been called a midget. He is dressed in a somber navy suit. Combined with the elaborate Orientalist décor of the restaurant, they and the other guests lend the evening the air of a debauched carnival.

At the end of the meal, Paul tells me that I should ask the waiter Aziz for a *"twiza."* By the looks on everyone's faces, I can see that he is trying to get me to do something foolish. Eventually, they tell me that *twiza* is an Arabic word meaning group sex. I note the similarity between the words *twiza* and *tazi,* and we joke that, given Paul's experiences there in the past, I may in fact be staying at the Grand Hotel Twiza.

Disco music plays from the stone vestibule of the restaurant, and Nourdine asks me if I want to dance. At first I'm confused, as this is not a gay club, but then I remember that dancing with men is permitted, and so Nourdine, Mohammed, and I head to the vestibule. We are joined occasionally by a handful of different women, none of whom can manage to talk their stuffy French escorts into dancing with them. Nourdine is a fabulous dancer, completely at ease and not afraid to flirt with me in public.

It is hot, and so I strip off my shirt to reveal a black lycra tank top, the kind of shirt I would never wear in the streets of Marrakech or even in most restaurants at home. For once, being the only American feels absolutely freeing. Because I am a foreigner, I don't have to worry about what other people think of me. Not being able to understand what they are saying makes me immune to criticism. And unlike when I am in Europe, I don't feel as if I somehow have to make up for the bad behavior of other U.S. tourists. Knowing the lyrics to a dance tune is a way of showing off here, as everyone wants to be able to sing English pop songs correctly, and no one but my friends and the waiter know that I am a native speaker. I sing along with Whitney Houston and Cher, enjoying the fact that I can dance with another man in public in a straight bar without fear for my safety. Nourdine, Mohammed, and I dance late into the night.

# ✍ 16    Breaking the Community Structure

*Ramy Eletreby*

A general consensus among those who grow up in an Arab community in the United States is that no matter how many members exist, it is still incredibly small. Everyone knows everything about everyone: what one's career is, how many children one has, when one goes away on vacation. News travels at lightning speed and no one can get around it. Privacy does not really exist, because if you're not doing anything wrong, why should anything be kept hidden? It's all out in the open, which can be both good and bad. In times of difficulty, such as death or disease, the overwhelming support from everyone you know, and even from those you don't, can be exceptionally touching. However, in times of personal stress, it can get burdensome when one would rather be left alone.

I was raised in greater Los Angeles in an Islamic household by Egyptian parents who immigrated to the United States four years before I was born. Most of my parents' relatives live in California, so visits back to Egypt were few and far between throughout my life. It was easier for the last remaining family members in Egypt to visit us in California than for all of us to go back to Cairo to see them. Although the Southern California Arab Muslim community primarily consists of Egyptians, it features everyone from Syrians and Palestinians to Iraqis and Lebanese. I have no idea how many Egyptians live here and how many of those are Muslim, but I feel like I know them all, and I probably do. I have been to more weddings than I care to remember, usually having never met the bride or groom. It is a community in which conformity is assumed, if not encouraged, and professional careers are revered. Every young Egyptian Muslim, male or female, is expected to go to college to become a doctor, engineer, or

*Gay Travels in the Muslim World*
© 2007 by The Haworth Press, Inc. All rights reserved.
doi:10.1300/5481_16

Islamic scholar and be married by the time they are in their mid-twenties. Individualism and matters of identity do not count for much, and any time someone does act as an individual, it is seen as a negative Western influence. Unsurprisingly, being gay and an artist just screams nonconformity, a rotten banana that ruins the bunch.

For me, the realization of self, the understanding that I am inherently different and will not live up to the high standards set forth for me, came in 1996, when I was fifteen years old. The reality of my world was suddenly no longer consistent with the world imagined for me when a series of small, yet remarkable, events proved to challenge the social structure I was bound to.

In April of 1996, my sophomore year of high school, a few friends and I got tickets to see a new play by Oliver Mayer called *Blade to the Heat* at Los Angeles's Mark Taper Forum, a place notorious for producing socially conscious and innovative pieces. Set in 1959, in a city similar to Los Angeles, the play was about professional Latino and black fighters, loosely based on a legendary boxing match that ended in murder due to homophobia.

Something magical happened to me that night. Being an exceptionally naive fifteen-year-old when it came to theater and political and social commentary, the themes of homophobia and the stereotypical Latin machismo went somewhat over my head. But on that profound night, my love for the theater fully blossomed. The extraordinarily creative piece just enthralled me. Its brilliant, stylized staging of the boxing matches as heightened dance pieces topped with Mayer's smooth and poetic text about the sheer theatricality and beauty of the sport forced me to see the theater as a transcendental experience. It was clear to me then that this is what I wanted to do with my life. I was no longer going to be a doctor as I had always expected to be. To my parents' disappointment, I told them the next day about my life's passion, and, true to form, the community knew instantly that they had lost one of their kids to the artistic world. If they knew what else happened that night, my career choice would have been the least of their worries.

A particular scene in *Blade to the Heat* caused me to examine another part of my identity and my future as an adult Muslim man. One of the boxers had a scene that took place in the locker room showers. I could not believe my eyes as this man naturally took off his boxing robe and his shorts and stood there naked under the showers, all the while having a conversation about boxing. How could someone do something so inherently private as showering publicly on stage and pretend its nothing? I had never seen a naked man before. I was shocked. I was flushed. I enjoyed it immensely. It was the epitome of beauty. The rawness, the casualness, the naturalness of it all just overwhelmed me. I realized fully for the first time that this was a huge part of who I am. I had prior inclinations and curiosity, but after seeing that beautiful act, I consciously knew the truth. It was in me. How was I going to be married to a nice Egyptian Muslim girl and have a family now? I was going to keep this to myself for a while. I had to find a way to survive this.

With my newly discovered sense of identity, it was time to do some work in reconciling my Eastern culture with my Western ideology. I believed that if I immersed myself in my history, then I would be able to find a way in which these two seemingly conflicting selves can co-exist, because I was certain they could. What better way to reclaim your foundation than by going back to the source? At that point, I hadn't been back to Egypt in five years, since I was ten years old. It was about time. That summer I went with my father and my uncle to Cairo for two weeks to attend a cousin's wedding. We three served as the ambassadors of the twenty-plus family members living in the United States. I was determined to take this trip as an opportunity to immerse myself in what it means to be a young Muslim Egyptian man. I tried to speak, in my broken Arabic, to as many people as possible to convince them and myself that I am a part of them. I danced till 4:00 a.m. I drank sugarcane juice. I rode a camel around the pyramids. I sailed down the Nile river on an entertainment boat with live Arabic music and belly dancing. I bartered in the streets for scarves, prayer rugs, and a marble chess board. I prayed with the locals in the mosque on Fridays. My being gay and an artist could, and should, not jeopardize all that. In fact, it seemed to me that the youth culture in Cairo was more liberal than the Egyptian culture in Los Angeles. Young women would party in sleeveless tops and short skirts, with their hair freshly done from the salon. No Egyptian Muslim parent I knew back home would let their daughter out of the house looking like that. I started to think that maybe all my concerns were for naught. If anything, in order to exist, I would just move to Cairo where I was sure I would be accepted. I had heard rumors that there were underground discotheques all across the city where gay and lesbian Egyptians would get together and revel in their existence. It all seemed fine. Going back to Egypt gave me the clarity I needed to feel confident in my ability to survive in the community I was raised in and still be true to myself. I would still keep this part of me a secret until I was old enough to responsibly make the decisions I needed to ensure my survival. I haven't been to Egypt since, but until four years ago, I was content with what I found.

When the Cairo 52 incident happened in May of 2001, I had just turned twenty and was in New York City as part of a college program. I had taken the opportunity of being away from home to start exploring my sexual identity when I read that fifty-two men were arrested on the Queen Boat, a gay discotheque on the Nile, for crimes of debauchery. All the security I felt, the idea that I may perhaps find an outlet for true expression, was immediately destroyed. What happened? Wasn't it Cairo that made me feel better about being who I was? Was it all just a misconception because I was a young teenager who could still not comprehend the complexity of society? The free and open Cairo that I naively witnessed no longer existed, if it ever did. The iron fist came down, and now gay men and women across the Arab Islamic world were in fear for their freedom. What was I to do now? I wasn't sure if I could own being gay anymore if it meant being persecuted by the Arab Islamic community.

The freshness of what happened in Cairo proved to inhibit my experience when I went to Turkey with my parents, aunt, and brother the next month in June. I had fully intended to use my time in Turkey to explore more actively the underground gay lifestyle in a primarily Islamic country. Istanbul is a lively city, with some of the most architecturally impressive mosques in the world, but after the recent high profile display of homophobia in the Islamic world, I felt an overwhelming sense of fear and insecurity about seeking out any gay spots. I no longer felt comfortable in the Islamic world as myself. I would have to be someone different if I wanted to survive. I have not visited an Islamic country since.

Since then, it became clear that this is not something I can escape. I cannot hide underground and live my life in fear, whether it is fear of imprisonment in the Eastern Islamic world or fear of social rejection in the Western Islamic world, my world in California. I have no choice but to stay in the United States and battle the community I grew up in. I have no choice but to challenge the conformist structure. I may be thought of as a rotten banana or a rebel, but at least I will have my freedom.

# Morocco

*Arch Brown*

Fatigued. Fogged in. Fagged out. After more than twelve hours of being squashed into a coach seat, I was bleary-eyed and barely functional. Cal, my partner, was in only slightly better shape, having slept for a few hours. We somehow stumbled down the gangway and across the dusty tarmac. As we entered the terminal a small man in a rumpled linen suit and straw fedora held up a sign with our names on it. He was extremely polite as he introduced himself, and taking our elbows, steered us through the throngs. He babbled on in his barely comprehensible English and fawned all over us as if we were visiting royalty. But his clear insincerity, condescending smirk, and averted eyes made his emotions clear. Did he think we had no sense of perception? He couldn't have cared less about us. It was only our tourist dollars that kept him focused. It was a look we would see again and again as the trip progressed—condescension mixed with sleazy charm.

He led us to the pile of luggage and helped us quickly get through customs. We climbed into his tiny Fiat that needed a good detailing. I couldn't sit up straight without hitting the roof, so I tried to sprawl at an angle that made me look more comfortable. I could have complained, or tried to move to the front seat next to him, but as always, I kept my mouth shut. No matter how low someone else was on the totem pole of life, I can always manage vague subservience.

We were informed that tomorrow we would have a free day to rest at our hotel, but on Monday he and his bumper car would pick us up at ten in the morning for our tour of the souk. Cal and I looked at each other in the simultaneous disbelief that we were the only two people on the tour and we would be spending most days with Mr.

*Gay Travels in the Muslim World*
© 2007 by The Haworth Press, Inc. All rights reserved.
doi:10.1300/5481_17

Mahmud. Not exactly what we had been looking forward to for our first visit to North Africa.

We had tried to enter Morocco in the late sixties. We had been on a self-drive tour of Spain, and on the spur of the moment had decided to take the car ferry across to Ceuta, a small Spanish colony on the North African coast. Without reservations, it was not easy finding a place for the night, but we eventually found a cheap, concrete-walled hotel room with no heat or hot water. The following morning we drove the three miles to the border with Morocco.

The border guards were not used to English speakers coming through from Ceuta, and the next five minutes were translation hell. When a supervisor was finally called over to our car, he explained that the guards had decided we looked like drug smugglers and we would be let into the country only if I allowed them to cut my hair. Just mine, not Cal's. This made no sense at all. Our hair was about the same length and cut to above the collars of our shirts. Granted, Cal's hair looked shorter because it was curly, but I certainly didn't have a hippie look, and neither of us had any drugs—or bead necklaces—on us. As the haggling went on it became clear there was no point in arguing. It was obvious they were toying with the disgustingly stupid Americans, and we were never going to win. So, swearing under his breath, Cal turned the car around and we took the ferry back to Spain. It made me furious that we had been turned back and managed to rationalize it only by repeating over and over that "I'll spend my money in some other damn country that wants it."

I was disappointed more than angry. It had been my suggestion that we cross the Pillars of Hercules because I had always been fascinated by North Africa, which was defined in my head by those Arabian fantasies that starred Errol Flynn and Virginia Mayo. The vision of white-bread John Agar in a turban as a handsome and charming Ali Baba who always managed to rescue the beautiful girl was deeply carved in the Memorex of my mind. So, when Cal was recently informed at the hospital that he had two weeks of vacation time that he had to use up by the end of the year, I was thrilled to find a cheap trip with one week in Marrakech and one week in Agadir on the Atlantic coast.

I hoped Mr. Mahmud was not typical of his countrymen; he certainly was not handsome, nor charming. Neither was the hotel's desk clerk. He spoke English well enough, but with a French, not a Moroccan, accent. We would soon learn that the hotel catered to mostly French tourists, and we were the only guests who each had only a high school level of comprehension of the language. I prayed this was not going to be more work than vacation.

Our room was small, but handsomely furnished. The pale taupe walls were a perfect background for the brightly woven fabrics of the upholstery and bedspreads. We also had a tiny balcony that overlooked the pool where sunbathers wore the smallest of bikinis and most women were topless. Yes, this was definitely a French destination.

We had learned from previous trips across the pond that it was essential to stay awake till at least after dinner before hitting the sack, in order to be even somewhat functional the next day. It was about four in the afternoon, local time, when we finished unpacking, and we decided to walk to the main square, Djamaa el Fna, which we knew from our guidebook was only a few blocks north.

As we exited the hotel we were swarmed by dozens of men, young and old, promising us the best of tours, rug dealers, jewelry shops, and restaurants. None seemed to have a badge *or* a car. Several followed us for blocks. Others grabbed us by the elbow and attempted to steer us down a side street or into a shop. In my jet-lagged state I couldn't handle any of it and finally screamed a long list of obscenities in English, which they all finally seemed to understand.

We were finally alone, and enthralled by the painted houses with lopsided doors and iron grates. The badly paved streets were dusty and crowded with locals, many on bikes, wearing everything from contemporary Western clothes to gauzy djellabas. You could smell the cumin and garlic seemingly wafting from every door. This was real, not a Hollywood fantasy.

We passed the La Mamounia Hotel, a luxury joint I was familiar with from travel books and Moroccan guide books. We entered slowly, not sure if we were trespassing and would be thrown out on our asses. No one bothered us. The people we presumed were staff smiled and nodded. Some even seemed sincere. The lobby and main hallways were decorated with gilt art deco carvings, marble, and hanging lamps glowing in many colors. The carpets alone were probably worth more than our Brooklyn brownstone. The intense luxury was a surreal contrast to the poor beggars and gritty air just outside. We checked out the menu for the main restaurant and wandered about the grounds and the pool terrace. We vowed to come back for lunch one day this week.

As we headed toward the Djamaa, the streets were even more of a bustle. The dust filled our eyes and lungs. We talked about how incredibly handsome so many of the younger men were, but that the older men seemed to have fallen apart by age thirty. As I was motioning Cal to check out an incredibly handsome guy on a bike, the rider caught my eye and headed straight at us.

He was a stunner. Pale skinned and dark haired, his features were the perfect vision of a Movie-Moroccan. His light and somehow translucent eyes were hazel and green and gray, all at the same time. He pulled his bike up on the splintered sidewalk and said, with a smile, *"Francais?"*

"No," I answered. "Americans."

"Ah, yes. I talk English good. Where are from?"

"New York City," Cal said with more grand affectation than I think he intended.

"Very tall city. I love to see all of USA, but most New York."

"It's a nice city," I said casually.

"You need guide. I am good guide. What you want see? Rug shops? Souvenirs shop? Jewelry for your wife?"

"We have a guide. We just wanted to walk to the square," Cal said politely.

I added, "We just arrived today. Too tired to tour today."

"Tomorrow then? What hotel you stay at? I am best guide in all Marrakesh. Ask anyone about Jamal."

"No, we already have a guide for tomorrow," Cal stated again.

"We're on a package vacation," I said, hoping to make a point.

"What a package?"

"We paid already for room, meals, and guides," Cal stated as if this explained everything.

But it didn't. It only seemed to confuse Jamal more. "Everyone need a guide. Everyone need Jamal."

I wondered if he knew what he was implying? He wasn't flirting or trying to be sexual in any apparent way. I was sure he had no clue.

"Thank you for the offer," I said cooly.

"But no guide better than me. I am best and know all about everything."

"But we don't need a guide," I said as strongly as I dared without insulting him.

"Then I take you on a tour now of El Fna. I know best tea shop and fakirs."

"No thank you," I said angrily.

"Just let me show you how good guide I am. I ride along while you walk," he said in tone that was mildly threatening. He obviously was not going to give up on us. I have always hated people forcing their way into my consciousness and I answered, "Just go away!"

"Why you be mean? I good guide."

"It doesn't matter," I said dismissively. "We will not pay you anything, so just go on your way."

Cal was strangely silent. He could often be more aggressive or argumentative than I, but he seemed to have given up this battle.

Jamal was suddenly charming again, perhaps even making himself available.

"I go with you now. You no pay me much. If you like me, I will meet you tomorrow for tour."

"But we already have a guide for tomorrow."

"But not as good like me."

"We've told you, we've already paid for another guide. Just leave us alone."

He was suddenly angry, his mouth curling into disgust. "You Americans have good money. I show you how good I am and you use me."

"We can't. We have to use the guide from the travel company."

"What hotel you at? I come tomorrow and guide you. You see I am best!"

"I don't care if you are, which I doubt. We simply will not do business with you. Please just leave us alone." He leaned closer into my face and sneered.

"You dumb. You not know how good guide I can be."

"Maybe you are, but just go. I don't want to deal with you under any deal. Just go!"

"You make deal now for another day?"

"No we can't and we won't. And step back, please."

"What you not like about Jamal? I am handsome and smart. Why you afraid? I no hurt you."

"Good. Then just leave us alone! You're not going to make any deal with us. Just get back on your bike and go!"

"You cheap tourist. You go home. Back to where you belong!"

"I will, as soon as we can. Now you just leave us alone."

"You hate Morocco! I see in your face. I go! And you go too, back to your New York." He pulled himself back, stared into my eyes, and spat in my face, just missing my left eye. The glob landed on my cheek and as I reached for my hankie. I took Cal by the arm and steered us down the street toward the square. Jamal was still following by ten feet.

"I can't deal, Cal, lets go back to the hotel."

"But he'll follow us there too. Just keep walking and pay no mind. He'll give up eventually."

"I doubt it. Please let's go back."

"You go if you want. I'm not going to let some asshole screw with my vacation." I couldn't believe I was being shunted off, dismissed. Cal never went his own way. He could be strong and was clever debating a subject he cared about, but at his core he's a bigger sissy than I am. Just more imperious.

"Where will you go?" I asked in lover-bashed anger.

"To the square. At least one of us will be free of him. Go ahead. I can see how upset you are. You're tired and cranky and—"

"Cranky? You think I'm overreacting to him, the whole situation?"

"Go back and have a drink. I'll be back in half an hour. Just don't fall asleep." He walked away, leaving me to do the only thing I could, turn on my heel and march home. When I passed Jamal, who was still following, I pretended I was looking up at some second-story window. Our eyes never met.

I walked as casually and as quickly as I could. After a few minutes I managed to stop to look at the reflection in a store window. Jamal was not behind me. Nor could I see him among the bicycling throngs on the road.

I did go back to the room, had a glass of wine, and sat watching a couple of French hunks teasing their big-boobed girlfriends by the pool. Why had I been so wigged out by Jamal? Was I simply afraid? Was I too damned attracted? Or was I just too exhausted to deal with that kind of invasion. What the hell was it all about? I'm a pretty self-aware guy. But I was scared shitless of something and needed Errol or John or Cornel Wilde to save me.

Cal didn't get back for over an hour. It turned out Jamal had given up and followed neither of us. When I asked him what the square was like, he answered, "Crowded and filthy and wonderful. I won't spoil it for you. We'll go back some other day. There are even second-floor cafés where you can watch the carryings on. You'll get the hang of not letting the touts bother you, although I almost smacked a guy who literally tried to drag me into his shop. I had to really struggle to get loose."

"And this is what we have to deal with? Day after day?"

Cal smiled broadly. "You're the one who wanted to come here."

"So now we're going to play blame games?"

"Not at all. But we gotta make the best of it that we can. You've survived your mother all these years. You'll get through the week just fine."

And we did survive the endless hawking and grabbing. I learned a sharp elbow in the ribs helped a lot. But I hated the daily battle for my sanity and safety. I've never gone back.

# ॐ18        Dust

*Steve Dunham*

Dust. Despite all other beautiful memories and evocative scenes, that one word conjures up Egypt. Sometimes reddish, sometimes golden, it was everywhere, indoors and out.

A few years ago, my longtime partner Rich and I joined a small college alumni group, no more than twenty people, to experience Egypt. It was an off time when we were sure to encounter only Europeans and maybe a few gaggles of camera-pointing Japanese. We flew from wintery New York to Paris, then on to balmy Luxor.

What Christian individual, no matter how agnostic later in life, doesn't retain vivid childhood images of Egypt gleaned from Sunday school illustrations of Moses in the bulrushes, attended by bejeweled, black-wigged princesses, and what museum worth its salt doesn't have a gloomy, lotus-columned chamber resplendent in glimmering cases full of unearthed tidbits, precious and mundane, along a crusty mummy or two?

It is all still there along the Nile, juxtaposed with jarring accouterments of contemporary life perhaps similar to that glimpsed by soldiers in Iraq today, when they have time to look. Except that Egypt was tranquil, dignified, only vaguely threatening. The cobra in the basket.

Each morning, upon opening the curtains and French windows to the balcony of our room in the quaint old Winter Palace Hotel, there it was on the glass tabletops: fresh new dust. Awakened by the rasping, loud-speakered prayer calls from the city's forest of minarets, we'd head for the pool but balk at the edge. The water was fifty-five degrees Fahrenheit and only hunky blond Swedes in wetsuits would dive in.

*Gay Travels in the Muslim World*
© 2007 by The Haworth Press, Inc. All rights reserved.
doi:10.1300/5481_18

The lavish Victorian lobby of the Winter Palace sported pert little honey-skinned young men in silk turbans, carrying gongs and salvers of messages for Lady Crumley, or whomever.

It was very hard not to notice these young men, and their lithe older brothers who often met them at night when they were leaving to go home. Rich and I believed ourselves to be the only gay fellows in our little clan, all others being married professors, doctors, or history buffs, but who knows? One striking younger guy, Gregg, was very friendly but had a witchy wife who watched his every move. Gregg in particular was amused by our severely Islamic and scholarly head guide Mohammed's biting wit. Mohammed repeatedly referred to Queen Hatshepsut, a warrior-like early example of take-charge woman, as "a pushy broad."

En route to Queen Hat's vast palace at Dandera, miles into the remote countryside, our little Volkswagen bus was guarded fore and aft by armored machine-gun cars. It was a period when the occasional bus of tourists would be butchered by what the media called religious fanatics. This was all during the time of the Achille Lauro, and the infamous brutal murder of an old man in a wheelchair which was splashed all over the evening news.

Along the way to Danderra, Technicolor scenes from moldy stacks of *National Geographic* came to life: burros and camels outnumbered the few old Citroens and Datsun trucks we passed. Mothers knelt by the river kneading the family wash on smooth ancient stones, their kids in little gowns and American baseball caps, frolicking in the water—with scads of monkeys! We Westerners were admonished not to stick even a toe into the pretty but poisonous (to us) Nile, and to avoid a long list of the artistically arrayed foods offered at each meal, and to drink only beer. Some of our physician colleagues scoffed, ate, and got very sick.

Boarding a splendid if garishly appointed touring yacht, the *Cleopatra,* we cruised for an idyllic week up the Nile, our eventual destination the giant Ramses figures at Abu Simbel. Landing now and then to explore, we perused the Old Kingdom, the New Kingdom, the edge of Nubia, in slow motion, without looking back. The pyramids, which you can creep up inside of; the nearly faceless Sphinx; the cow-headed columns of the earth goddess's temple; the shrine full of crocodile mummies.

Lounging on the top deck under a white duck awning, watching the rainbow-hued, domed villages and coffee-colored inhabitants go by was a priceless time warp. Even in Cairo, city of seventeen million, only business people wore European clothing.

The dark-eyed, sinewy young waiters and cabin boys were beguiling, and were good candidates for what Rich and I call "storytelling" in bed. Our stateroom had slender twin bunks and a mirrored ceiling. We imagined the possibilities.

But we didn't try anything. All of us know plenty about the obsession of generations of gay male Western travelers for wily Mediterranean lads. They've written of it, filmed it, poeticized it, and done it in the flesh ad nauseam. Romantic as it sounds, the simple truth is that sexy youths from underprivileged backgrounds anywhere will do anything for money—even in Peoria.

During New Year's Eve in the dining saloon, the waiters and musicians donned bizarre makeup and scanty getups to entertain us with a rousing parade among the tables, banging big pots and kitchen tools to wild Middle Eastern disco music. Next came gorgeous belly dancers, but the big treat for Rich and me was the dervish—a young, androgynous creature who whirled and whirled to demonic rhythms, faster and faster until he fainted and was carried aloft from the room.

The most wonderful thing about all the Egyptians we came close to, even the machine-gun toting, godlike young sentries on Cairo street corners, was their smell. Even if low on the economic ladder, they remained well-groomed. Yet it was not the fragrance of the boutique but something everyday—maybe simply the aroma of clean skin.

On our coffee table at home is a little round silver box embossed with a pharaoh's visage, bought at the Egyptian Museum in Cairo. It contains sand we reverently gathered at the doorway down to King Tut's tomb, with the bemused permission of a smiling elderly guard, pistol barely visible under his kaftan.

King Tut, hah! This was the sole disappointment of the journey, realized months later after reading columnist Liz Smith's autobiography, in which she reports that she was one of the last outsiders to clamber into King Tut's *real* tomb. For reasons of both security and preservation, wrote Liz, a suitable nearby replica has been fashioned for the rubes of the world. It was a letdown, like Plymouth Rock or the Easter Bunny, but at least that silver box looks good and opens up a conversation!

Most alluring of the places we explored was Alexandria. Curling along the Mediterranean like an alabaster scimitar, it exactly mirrors its counterpart, Nice, across the way in Europe, but was faded and shabby. I kept thinking of the city in Lawrence Durrell's *The Alexandria Quartet,* which I read as a teenager, and which gripped my soul even then because of its suppressed homoerotic currents.

Alexandria reminded us of Miami Beach of the 1940s, blandly bordering the sea with an endless wall of creamy deco villas, apartments, and hotels. The backstreets and hilltops are a tapestry of French colonial, Greek, and Roman flotsam. At the very eastern tip are the gardens of King Farouk, the fat and famous barfly.

Heading back to Cairo on the arrow-straight freeway, across utterly empty desert, we paused at what in the United States would be a turnpike oasis—gas pumps, restrooms, coffee shop, souvenirs. Unlike in New Jersey, however, the place was shiny and immaculate, hermetically sealed off from its sandy ocean. The building was cubic and glassy, the a décor striking red, yellow, black, and white. Splendidly uniformed attendants solemnly bowed low to welcome us to Modern Egypt.

We used the restrooms but purchased nothing, for we were headed to a gala farewell feast at Cairo's glitzy Nefertiti Hotel, presumably safe for our delicate American stomachs.

A little ashamed, we left the glass confines and retreated back into the dust, this time tinged a curious, baleful beige by the setting sun.

# About the Editor

**Michael Luongo, MCRP,** is Senior Editor of The Haworth Press' "Out in the World" Gay Travel Literature series. A New York-based travel writer and photographer with experience in 75 countries and all seven continents, he has written for *The New York Times,* the *Chicago Tribune, Conde Nast Traveler, National Geographic Traveler,* the *Advocate, Out Traveler, Passport,* and many other publications. Mr. Luongo has written or edited several travel books, including *Frommer's 2005 Buenos Aires, Gay Tourism: Culture, Identity and Sex,* and Haworth's *Between the Palms,* a collection of gay travel erotica. Visit him at www.michaelluongo.com.

*Gay Travels in the Muslim World*
© 2007 by The Haworth Press, Inc. All rights reserved.
doi:10.1300/5481_19

# Contributors

**Joe Ambrose** is a DJ and member of experimental hip-hop group Islamic Diggers. He and Frank Rynne produced the CD *10 Percent: File Under Burroughs,* featuring Joujouka, Marianne Faithfull, John Cale, and William S. Burroughs. In 1992 Ambrose and Rynne did *The Here to Go Show,* a celebration of the wild cultural experimentation of William S. Burroughs and Brion Gysin. Collaborators on this included Iggy Pop and Hamri the Painter of Morocco. His books include two novels, *Serious Time* and *Too Much Too Soon,* and book titled *Moshpit Culture,* an investigation of covert punk culture. His next book, *Chelsea Hotel Manhattan,* comes out with Headpress in 2007. Ambrose is Literary Editor of www.outsideleft.com. He divides his time between London, his native Ireland, and Morocco. You can visit him at www.joeambrose.net.

**Richard Ammon** is a former psychologist, teacher, and carpenter, and is now a full-time slave to his Web site www.GlobalGayz.com as writer, photographer, and Webmaster. He welcomes stories about LGBT life from all over the world.

**Desmond Ariel** lives a quiet life, mostly alone. He travels sometimes, but not much anymore. A recent story, "Twelve Days in a Week," appeared in *Foreign Affairs* (2004, Cleis Press). He has written in other guises, publishing reviews, journalism, essays, and fiction. He is working slowly on a novel, with work due to appear in other Haworth Press books as well.

**Don Bapst** is the author of four plays, two collections of poetry, and three novels, including *Posthumous Timeline,* from which "Winter,

*Gay Travels in the Muslim World*
© 2007 by The Haworth Press, Inc. All rights reserved.
doi:10.1300/5481_20

1995" has been excerpted. He has written for numerous publications and is a regular contributor to *blue* magazine. Born in Chicago, where he currently resides, he has lived in London, Paris, Ouagadougou, New York, and San Francisco. You can visit him online at www .donbapst.com.

**Thomas Bradbury** is a pseudonym for a New York travel agent who specializes in Turkey. He changed his name to protect the innocent, and the guilty.

"I dedicate this story to all my wonderful friends in Turkey, who have renewed and changed my life in ways I could never imagine."

**Arch Brown's** essays and reviews have appeared in the *Advocate*, the *Villager, Manhattan Gaze*, and he had a regular column on "Television and Society" in the *New York Native*. In memory of Bruce Brown who died in 1993 he sponsors The Arch and Bruce Brown Foundation, which gives grants to gay-positive arts projects. Arch's double biography of his twenty-eight-year relationship with Bruce was published in *Longtime Companions* by Haworth Press. His films include *Four Letters, Pier Groups, The Tool Man, Dynamite! All Tied Up,* and *Sir Real.* His film *Tuesday* was the only gay film included by the New York Erotic Film Festival in its nationwide release. His published and/or produced plays include *News Boy, Sex Symbols, Brut Farce, Seeing Red,* and *Ships That Piss in the Night.* Brown's play, *FREEZE!* won the 1998 Eric Bentley New Play Competition. Brown is a voting member of The Dramatists Guild.

**John Champagne** is an Associate Professor of English at Penn State Erie, the Behrend College. He is the author of three novels, *The Blue Lady's Hands, Lyle Stuart,* and *When the Parrot Boy Sings,* as well as a work of cultural criticism, *The Ethics of Marginality: A New Approach to Gay Studies.* His poems, personal essays, and scholarly prose have appeared in such journals as *The Journal of Homosexuality, Kenyon Review, Harrington Gay Men's Fiction Quarterly,* and *College English.*

**Jay Davidson** taught in San Francisco public schools from 1969-2003. Upon his retirement he joined the Peace Corps and was assigned to the Islamic Republic of Mauritania, where he served for two years as a Curriculum Development Specialist, writing English textbooks and teaching English to adults. In San Francisco, he was a founding member and first general manager of the San Francisco Gay Men's Chorus, as well as founder and first president of the Gay and Lesbian Association of Choruses. He is the author of *Teach Your Children Well: A Teacher's Advice for Parents,* as well as booklets about stress reduction, socially responsible travel, and guiding children to success in school. Information about his writing is available at www.jay davidson.com.

**Steve Dunham** is a contributor to Michael Luongo's volume of gay travel tales, *Between the Palms,* published by The Haworth Press. Recent publishers of Steve's work include Alyson, AuthorHouse, and *Genre Magazine,* for which he garnered a National Magazine Award. After three decades of journalism and government service he has developed a favorite specialty: fiction derived from personal experiences, from comical to diabolical—the perfect description of his new novella, *Cleopatra's Tomb,* not yet published. Steve and his longtime partner reside in Savannah and Chicago.

**Ramy Eletreby** was born and raised in the Los Angeles area, where he currently lives as a journalist and an actor. He writes for *IN Los Angeles Magazine,* for which he serves as a news reporter and social columnist. He attended the University of California, Irvine, and earned bachelor's degrees in both drama and English. Throughout his life Ramy has been heavily involved in the local Muslim community, including helping to organize three consecutive annual youth retreats. As an actor, Ramy recently performed the role of Tameem in the Cornerstone Theater Company's world premier play, *A Long Bridge Over Deep Waters.* Ramy is also a member of the Uprising Theatre Company, having appeared in their productions of *Hamlet* and *Macbeth.* He has trained at the Professional Conservatory at South Coast Repertory and past productions include *The Skin of our Teeth, The Good Person of*

*Szechwan,* and *The Prince.* His Web site has more information on his work: www.ramyeletreby.com

**Martin Foreman** was born in the UK and has lived at various times of his life in Greece, Brazil, and the United States. He has also traveled widely, and currently lives in Bangkok where he spends part of the time running a tour company. Martin's writings encompass a wide range of themes. He has had two novels and two collections of short stories published, as well as several studies on HIV/AIDS in the developing world. A selection of his work can be seen on www.mart inforeman.com and www.godwouldbeanatheist.com.

**Afdhere Jama** is a Somali-born writer and activist. He is the editor of *Huriyah,* a queer Muslim magazine, and the author of the forthcoming *Queer Muslims,* a book of essays about Muslims all over the world struggling to reconcile their sexuality with their faith. His articles have appeared in many publications, including *DIVA* magazine (UK), *Zero* magazine (Spain,) *Behind the Mask* (South Africa) and *Arise Magazine* (U.S.) and many others. Although he is a nomad who has lived all over the world, he currently pays rent in San Francisco.

**Jeff Key** served as a U.S. Marine in the Iraq war. Upon returning to the United States, he went on CNN and came out of the closet to five million people and spoke out against the war, thereby using the ban on gays in the U.S. military to be discharged and stay true to his convictions. His play, *The Eyes of Babylon,* was developed from his personal journals from Iraq, and continues to tour the Unites States and other countries. Jeff Key and the play is the subject of a documentary on the Showtime Network slated to be aired in the Fall of 2007. Jeff is also the founder of the Mehadi Foundation, a nonprofit organization in support of the veterans of this war and philanthropic efforts in Iraq (http://MehadiFoundation.org). It is to these people, the veterans of the Iraq war and the noble people of Iraq, that his contributions to this work are dedicated.

**David C. Muller** was originally born in Virginia, but has lived in Japan, England, Italy, Morocco, the United States, and Australia. Currently he lives on a kibbutz somewhere in Israel. His writing has appeared in English in *David Atlanta* magazine, and *The Atlanta Journal-Constitution*. His fictional series, *Peachtree Passions,* was also published in *David Atlanta* magazine under the pen name "Day Day Los Angeles."www.davidatlanta.com Most recently, his story "I Met God Once" was published for the first time in English in Israel in a collection of short stories called *Shevet*. David holds a BA in political science from the University of Judaism in Los Angeles, California, and an MA in creative writing and English literature from Bar-Ilan University in Ramat-Gan.

**Ethan Pullman** was born to Palestinian parents and raised in various parts of the Middle East. He moved to the United States in his late teens, earned a degree in French, and later earned a degree in Library and Information Science. Currently, he works as a librarian and teaches Arabic at the University of Pittsburgh. He reviews for *Library Journal* and *Educational Media Reviews Online* in various disciplines such as international affairs and Middle Eastern and GLBT studies. This is his first short story.

"To my family of choice, the Pullmans, thank you for choosing me in return."

**Parvez Sharma** is a New-York based gay Muslim filmmaker who grew up in India and was educated in the UK and the United States. He worked for India's Star News channel, and on programming for BBC World Television (India), Central Television (UK), and the Discovery Channel (U.S.). He was a print journalist for several Indian newspapers including the *Telegraph* and the *Statesman*. At the *Statesman* he wrote the first article detailing the Indian lesbian experience. "Emerging from the Shadows" (July 3, 1994) became a rallying point for lesbians around India, and was crucial in the formation of many lesbian organizations. He has three master's degrees, including one in film and video from American University's School of Communication.

Parvez has launched a worldwide broadcast and activism project with his feature documentary *In the Name of Allah* (in progress)—the world's first documentary film on the complex intersections of Islam and homosexuality. In production for several now, the film is produced in association with Channel 4 Television (UK), ZDF (Germany), Arte (France), MTV's Logo (U.S.), and SBS (Australia). More on his work is at www.inthenameofallah.net.

**David Stevens** is a writer and teacher with a keen interest in Arab culture. Born in Sydney, he has lived in both Oman and Saudi Arabia, but calls Australia home between spells in the Middle East. He has traveled widely and contributed to a wide variety of publications— from the *Gay Australia Guide* to the *Sydney Morning Herald*. In the cities of Arabia he enjoys being woken by call of the muezzin for the dawn prayer, the aroma of *luban* (frankincense), and the tang of freshly brewed *shay bil na'na'* (mint tea).

**Rahal X** is an intercultural, multimedia artist, writer, and composer of Arab-Latino origin who has lived, worked, and exhibited in Germany, Spain, Latin America, Australia, the United States, Egypt, the United Arab Emirates, Portugal, Tunisia, and Morocco. Currently he lives between Marrakech and Berlin, where he is working on his book, *A Nomad's Patchwork,* to be published soon.